Tennisology

Inside the Science of Serves, Nerves, and On-Court Dominance

Thomas W. Rowland

Human Kinetics

Library of Congress Cataloging-in-Publication data has been applied for.

ISBN: 978-1-4504-6969-2 (print)

The web addresses cited in this text were current as of December 2013, unless otherwise noted.

Developmental Editor: Claire Marty; **Managing Editor:** Tyler Wolpert; **Copyeditor:** Mandy Eastin-Allen; **Indexer:** Laurel Plotzke; **Permissions Manager:** Martha Gullo; **Cover Designer:** Keith Blomberg; **Photograph (cover):** © Human Kinetics; **Photo Asset Manager:** Laura Fitch; **Photo Production Manager:** Jason Allen; **Art Manager:** Kelly Hendren; **Associate Art Manager:** Alan L. Wilborn; **Illustrations:** © Human Kinetics, unless otherwise noted; **Printer:** United Graphics

Human Kinetics books are available at special discounts for bulk purchase. Special editions or book excerpts can also be created to specification. For details, contact the Special Sales Manager at Human Kinetics.

Printed in the United States of America   10 9 8 7 6 5 4 3 2 1

The paper in this book is certified under a sustainable forestry program.

Human Kinetics
Website: www.HumanKinetics.com

United States: Human Kinetics
P.O. Box 5076
Champaign, IL 61825-5076
800-747-4457
e-mail: humank@hkusa.com

Canada: Human Kinetics
475 Devonshire Road Unit 100
Windsor, ON N8Y 2L5
800-465-7301 (in Canada only)
e-mail: info@hkcanada.com

Europe: Human Kinetics
107 Bradford Road
Stanningley
Leeds LS28 6AT, United Kingdom
+44 (0) 113 255 5665
e-mail: hk@hkeurope.com

Australia: Human Kinetics
57A Price Avenue
Lower Mitcham, South Australia 5062
08 8372 0999
e-mail: info@hkaustralia.com

New Zealand: Human Kinetics
P.O. Box 80
Torrens Park, South Australia 5062
0800 222 062
e-mail: info@hknewzealand.com

E6177

This book is dedicated to the memory of my parents, Dr. A. Westley Rowland and Belle Rowland, who instilled in their eldest son the lifelong joy of playing the game of tennis.

CONTENTS

PREFACE

This book that you are holding in your hands was 51 years in the writing.

It started on May 21, 1963. An earnest young reporter from the University of Michigan school paper, *The Michigan Daily*, was sharing lunch with Ray Senkowski, the Wolverines' best hope for a Big Ten singles tennis title, at a restaurant in Evanston, Illinois.

> Senkowski: Tennis is the most amazing sport.
>
> Reporter: Uh-huh.
>
> Senkowski: Just the way the game flows. Each point is like a short story, one which you don't know the ending.
>
> Reporter: Yeah.
>
> Senkowski: You know, I can tell all about a person— what he's like—just after playing tennis against him for five minutes. Probably more than someone who's known him for many years.
>
> Reporter: Really?
>
> Senkowski: Have you ever thought about it? The game of tennis is really just like life.
>
> Reporter: Yeah.

The reporter demonstrating those keen investigative skills is, of course, this author. Briefly on the team as a freshman, a decision to switch to journalism had been rapidly made after being wiped out 6-0, 6-1 by former Canadian junior champion Harry Fauquier on the first day of practice. (Fauquier went on to lose to Roy Emerson in the opening round at Wimbledon two years later by a remarkably similar 6-2, 6-1, 6-0 score.

Was it mere coincidence or divine retribution? Late at night one still wonders.)

Senkowski was about to defend his Big Ten title that afternoon against Northwestern's Marty Riessen. Unsuccessfully, it turned out, when a net cord caused him to drop the second set. Ray had taken the first, 6-2, but his forehand tipped the top of the net and fell back, and with that his momentum. Just when victory had seemed so close at hand it was a straight meltdown, and Riessen took the title. So, as he said, it's just like life—an inch here, an inch there, and you're a champ or a loser.

Over the years Ray's idea keeps coming back to me. Does the game of tennis really mimic life? Sometimes it seems like going out there and batting the fuzzy ball across the net is just entertainment, and sometimes it is much more philosophically and metaphysically profound. In other words, what does tennis really *mean*?

There's no question that the game of tennis shares a great deal of what we experience in daily life. How we act (aggressive or passive), how we make decisions (both good and bad), and how we confront uncertainty, accept mistakes, and face winning and losing alike—it's all there on the court as well as in our daily routines. We can gain a good deal of insight about ourselves as well as the people we play, work, and live with during a set or two on a warm summer's afternoon.

But tennis is a lot of other things, too, such as philosophy, psychology, history, art, ethics, and—particularly—science. The technical advances in rackets, formulation of court playing surfaces, insight into proper practice regimens, development of game-appropriate training based on knowledge of physiology, physics that guides shot selection—the list is long. All of these have contributed to the essence of what the game has become.

This theme flows through the chapters of this book. Certainly those responsible for training the world's greatest tennis players have long relied on approaches based on insights from scientific research. The chapters that follow demonstrate that the average 3.5-ranked player at the club level can learn a good deal from this research as well.

Chapter 1 explores the historical roots of modern-day tennis and depicts how changes in the game reflect changes in the society in which the game is played. Present-day tennis competition bears little resemblance to the original game of *jeu de paume*, played indoors by pious personages in the cathedrals of 12th century Europe, or to the easy social ambiance of the courts on the lawns of the Victorian British elite. The history of tennis has been marked by the fascinating—and often controversial—personalities who have played and shaped the game. Just as important to the development of the sport are the contributions of science.

Chapter 2 considers how challenges on the court so closely reflect those faced in daily life. Perhaps the meaning of tennis lies in some inherent need to face possible frustration and defeat for the chance of success and victory, or maybe the social aspects of club membership, the joy of muscular movement, and the health benefits of tennis are sufficient to explain the draw of the sport.

Chapter 3 discusses just how the human body learns to play the game and examines the means by which one acquires the rather miraculous physical and mental skills that go into tennis play. The interesting basic neurophysiology presented in these pages has practical importance in how one might best learn, improve, and teach the game.

Is one's ability to play the game of tennis dictated by the genetic information inherited from parents? Or, instead, is one able to improve through hours of committed practice? Chapter 4 examines this age-old nature versus nurture argument, which has a particularly critical implication in sport. The genetic argument implies a ceiling above which one cannot improve, whereas the training argument suggests that there's always hope for steady improvement and that the control of progress is in the hands of the player.

Chapter 5 delves into a controversy that's an issue for both those raising tennis-playing children and coaches training young players. Some feel that youngsters should be directed into early sport specialization as a means of producing (ultimately) star performers. However, it may be more healthy—

and, in the end, more successful—to encourage well-rounded involvement in sport play and delay tennis specialization until the early teen years. Opinion on this issue might revolve around how one perceives the role of deliberate practice in producing elite-level athletes.

Tennis is a game of uncertainty that is played within a set of immutable rules, both designed (e.g., keeping the ball in the lines) and physical (e.g., the forces of physics). Chapter 6 reviews the physical laws that define the game and emphasizes that understanding the effects of gravity and spin on the ball can give players an advantage.

Chapters 7 and 8 discuss two topics influencing tennis-playing skill that are under the direct control of the individual player and that have changed the nature of the game. Technical advances in tennis equipment—particularly the racket—have dramatically altered how the game is played. These advances are available to everyone, from the senior player on the community tennis court to the Wimbledon finalist. Similarly, as the level of play has increased in all parts of the game, the role that physical fitness plays in determining winner versus loser has become apparent. These chapters discuss how players can take advantage of scientific knowledge in both technical advances and physical fitness.

New neurophysiologic information indicates that motor skills might be achieved, at least to some extent, by visually witnessing others perform a particular action, such as a serve or drop shot. This is a step beyond mentally imaging your own supreme performance, which is a traditional tool of sport psychologists. It's about your brain actually being able to imitate and learn the mechanics of Roger Federer's tennis serve simply by watching him perform it. Chapter 9 explores this fascinating new frontier.

No person who has ever competed on the tennis court is oblivious to the critical role that psychological factors—especially mental toughness—play in achieving winning success. Chapter 10 reviews the psychological constructs that define such mental hardiness and offers some ideas on how it might be achieved.

The chapters in this book provide insight into how myriad factors—psychological, physiological, and physical—combine to affect the game of tennis. In recognizing such influences, the tennis player—young or old, 2.5 or 5.5—will be able to enhance both the performance and enjoyment of a truly marvelous game.

One more theme runs through the chapters of this book. The challenge of tennis is not the weather, the racket, the court surface, or even the opponent. It's you. It couldn't be said more eloquently than David Foster Wallace wrote in *Infinite Jest:*

> The true opponent, the enfolding boundary, is the player himself. Always and only the self out there on the court, to be met, fought, brought to the table to hammer out terms. The competing boy on the net's other side: he is not the foe: he is more the partner in the dance. He is what is the word *excuse* or *occasion* for meeting the self. Tennis's beauty's infinite roots are self-competitive. You compete within your own limits to transcend the self in imagination and execution. Disappear inside the game: break through limits: transcend: improve: win . . . . All life is the same . . . the animating limits are within.[1]

CHAPTER 1

Evolution of the Sport

Just outside Birmingham, England, is the Barber Institute of Fine Arts, nestled among the majestic elms of the University of Birmingham. In the summer of 2011, the institute mounted a unique exhibition of the art of tennis called "Court on Canvas." The message was that tennis is indeed artful. It's a game of grace and rhythm that, to both players and spectators, undeniably has a true sense of beauty. It is powerful and dramatic and has the sensuousness of muscular effort.

In a fascinating way, artists depicting the game of tennis have expressed—purposefully or not—its place in the cultural milieu of human society. Visitors roaming the exhibit were struck by how these works displayed how the role of tennis has changed over time. These paintings did not simply address the artistic aspects of a physical contest; rather, they revealed tennis to be a sociological mirror. It is fascinating to see how the games we play—tennis, in this particular case—reflect the culture that surrounds us. We witness the changing roles of women in society, the ways social class evolves over time, and the influence of war, technology, and economic trends. They're all there in the evolution of the game.

This exhibit was presented at the Barber Institute of Fine Arts because the institute sits just under a kilometer from the Ampton Road address in Edgbaston where Augurio Perera in 1859 played the very first game of lawn tennis with his friend Harry Gem, making up the rules as they went along. This marked the beginning of the adoption of the game among the croquet-playing British leisure class.

The early paintings in the exhibit depicted lawn tennis as a fashionable, relaxed social pastime of upper-class men and women, who usually gathered about grassy tennis courts in the elaborate shaded gardens of country estates. It was a slow-moving game to be sure. Etiquette was broken, for instance, if one served overhand or sprinted to return a hard-hit ball. The exhibit guidebook, written by organizer Ann Sumner, includes an 1881 quote from Lieutenant Colonel Robert Olson describing the perfect setting for an afternoon of lawn tennis:

> The scene should be laid on a well-kept garden lawn. There should be a bright warm sun overhead, and just sufficient breeze whispering through the trees . . . to prevent the day from being sultry. Near at hand, under the cool shadow of a tree, there should be strawberries and cream, an iced claret mug, and a few spectators who do not want to play but are lovers of the game, intelligent and appreciative. If all these conditions are present, an afternoon spent at lawns tennis is a highly Christian and beneficent pastime.[8]

These Victorian-era paintings of lawn tennis in Great Britain focused almost exclusively on female players. Where were the men? Most often in the background. At the time, women participating in vigorous physical activity—particularly red-faced damsels running about a tennis court in mixed doubles in the heat of summer—were quite a novelty. Female involvement in tennis challenged the standards of the day, which held that such athletic play was a threat to femininity. Lawn tennis broke the traditional models of female behavior in what was exclusively a male-dominated society, particularly in sport. As evident from these early paintings, females were expected to play attired in full-length dresses, corsets, and hats— hardly conducive to a vicious serve-and-volley game.

The exhibit guidebook quotes Herbert Chipp, secretary of the Lawn Tennis Association in 1900:

> Whether for better or worse, whether we disapprove with our grandmothers or approve with our daughters, times have changed . . . We may surely venture to hope that our daughters will not be worse mothers because, instead of leading sedentary lives, a great proportion of their young years will be spent . . . on the tennis court.[8]

Early female tennis players, like French player Suzanne Lenglen, shown here hitting a forehand in 1923, helped break traditional conventions and signaled the coming growth of rights and freedoms for women.

Barratts/Press Association Images

Mr. Chipp could hardly have foreseen the role of women—and mothers—on the international stage in today's hard-paced game. Nor was it clear in 1900 that the development of females on the tennis court would foreshadow the growth of the rights and freedoms of women throughout Great Britain.

There is no mistaking the message of this exhibit: There is true beauty in the sport of tennis, the evolution of which has always been an expression of the society surrounding it. From the early days of its narrow status among the elite to becoming a popular sport enjoyed around the world, the game of tennis has always reflected social change.

Historical Origins

The historical roots of modern tennis go much deeper than the lazy, hazy afternoons of lawn tennis in 19th century Great Britain. As Patty Hurtado has written, it appears that humans have been attracted to swinging sticks at balls in the name of sport competition since antiquity.[5] However, the most direct ancestor of today's tennis is the game of *jeu de paume* ("game with the hand"), which was played in France as early as the 1100s. In this game, the ball, made of solid cork covered with leather strapping, was struck over a low-slung net or sometimes a narrow mound of earth, initially with the hands (as indicated by the name) and then eventually with short, curved rackets. The game was played in a narrow indoor hall with tall walls and high ceilings, and the most common adversaries were friars and monks in Middle Age monasteries.

The game spread throughout Europe and experienced particular growth in England, where it was called court tennis or real tennis. Here it was played largely by the nobility and was particularly popular with the British royalty. (It has been suggested that King Henry VIII, who was obsessed with the game, had more rackets than wives.) Given the high velocity of the solid ball, in playing this game one actually assumed a risk of demise in addition to the ignominy of defeat. In the 14th century, the brother of the French thinker Montaigne died after being hit in the head by a ball. This event seemed to alter Montaigne's fear of death; he decided, in the end, not to worry about it. In 1751, the Prince of Wales died from what may have been an infected wound caused by a ball strike to the abdomen.

Many tennis terms used today presumably originate from this time, particularly from France. Most agree that the term *love* is derived from the French *l'oeuf*, meaning a goose egg (i.e., zero). The word *tennis* itself probably originates from the French *tenez* (translated as "brace yourself"), which the server would shout before striking the ball. *Deuce* comes from *a deux*, indicating that the next player to win two consecutive points will take the game.

Growth of International Competition

The popularity of lawn tennis peaked in Great Britain in the mid-1930s, and by 1940 everything had changed. World War II was upon Europe, and gone were carefree afternoons spent on country estates. It marked the end of the golden era of British tennis, which was to be replaced by yet another revolution in the game: the development of international tennis competition.

By the 1920s the International Tennis Federation (ITF) stimulated this development by designating sites of international championships in Europe, the United States, and Australia. These Grand Slam events, eventually aided by television coverage, showcased the top stars of the game, and tennis became identified by the elite who battled it out for the championships at the majors: Wimbledon, Roland Garros, New York City, and Melbourne. Each event has its own unique personality and stories.[2]

Wimbledon

Not long after Perera and Gem laid out the first lawn tennis court in their back yard, private clubs formed throughout England and competitions were organized. One such championship meet was conducted in 1877 on a four-acre plot off Worple Road in Wimbledon, about eight miles (12.9 km) outside of central London. The evolution of tennis as an international competitive sport was underway.

Spencer William Gore won that first Wimbledon tournament, organized by the All England Croquet and Lawn Tennis Club. Gore achieved victory by employing the unusual —and now illegal—strategy of leaning over and striking his opponent's ball before it crossed the net. (It wasn't until six years later that a women's competition was added; Maud Watson took the singles title.)

It was the second Wimbledon, held the next year, that really captured the public's attention. Gore returned to defend his crown against Frank Hadow, who had just come back from his regular job of planting tea in Ceylon and who had taken up the sport of lawn tennis only a few weeks earlier. Hadow took the first two sets (7-5, 6-1) but tired as things became tight in the third. He found new life, though, by sailing the ball high over Gore's head. He took the third set 9-7 to win the title—and invented the lob in the process. Afterward, Hadow returned to Ceylon, never to compete at Wimbledon again, and Gore went back to his favorite sport: cricket.[1]

French Open

Across the Channel, tournaments that formed in the 1890s were precursors of the French Open. In 1925 the ITF designated the annual competition at the Stade Roland Garros, just off the Bois de Boulogne in Paris, to be a major championship. Here the competition was altogether different from that at Wimbledon because the tournament was played on a court surface that the gentry of Victorian England would have found insufferable: dirt, or, more accurately, *terre battue* ("red clay"). The surface of this court is a thin layer of brick and tile powder covering three inches (7.6 cm) of white limestone, which for the past 100 years has come from the same quarry at Saint-Maximin, north of Paris.

In addition to sticking to shoes and socks, the red clay slows the bounce of the ball and causes it to rise higher, thus accentuating the effect of topspin. Players who pounded powerful shots from the baseline and played a strong defensive game found this surface in Paris more to their liking than did those who relied on an aggressive serve-and-volley style.

Incidentally, Roland Garros (1888-1918) was not a tennis player but rather was a celebrated French aviator and World War I fighter pilot. He initially gained fame for being the first to fly nonstop across the Mediterranean Sea from southern France to Tunisia. Later, during the war, he developed a way to use metal deflector wedges to fire a machine gun forward from a fighter plane without damaging the propeller. (Before that time the usual approach was to take shots at the enemy plane with a rifle or revolver.) For these feats as well as his faithful attendance at the French Open when he was a student in Paris, the tennis center was named for him in 1920.

U.S. Open

The United States Tennis Association was created in 1881 and held its first national championship that same year on the grass courts of The Casino in Newport, Rhode Island. In 1915 the U.S. Open moved to the West Side Tennis Club in Forest Hills, New York, where it stayed for 63 years before moving to its current home at Flushing Meadows in Queens. The acrylic hard surface, which is fast and promotes a low bounce of the ball, is more attractive to players with a serve-and-volley style. Old-time tennis fans cannot help but remember the deafening roar of the wide-body jets as they used runway 13/31 at nearby LaGuardia Airport, sometimes as often as once a minute, and coursed directly over the tennis center during the Open. Somebody once said that this regular cacophony bothered only the players who were losing. Now all is quieter because air traffic controllers divert aircraft traffic to other patterns during the Open when weather conditions permit.

Australian Open

The fourth of the Grand Slam events, the Australian Open in Melbourne, was designated a major championship by the ITF in 1924. However, due to its remote location, it took some years before this tournament assumed an international flavor. At the time the tournament became sanctioned, it normally took more than a month and a half to reach Australia from Europe by boat. When Don Budge became the first player to achieve what was called a grand slam (defined as winning all four international championships in one year) in 1938, the sea journey from San Francisco to Melbourne lasted 21 days. It wasn't until 1946 that players arrived by air. The tournament down under turned high profile thanks to the development of jet airliners and international television coverage.

The courts at the Australian Open were originally grass, but the tournament changed to a hard court surface (Rebound Ace) when it found its current home at Melbourne Park in 1988. In 2008, this was replaced by an acrylic hard surface, which is similar to that used at the U.S. Open.

Changes in Style of Play

Anyone who is remotely acquainted with tennis recognizes that the game has dramatically transitioned from a leisurely, slow-moving contest to the powerful, high-adrenaline battle one witnesses on contemporary courts.[4] This is most striking in the speed and power seen in the elite play at the Grand Slam tournaments but is also observed at high school, university, and even club meets.

Before 1900, tennis was a leisurely pat-ball sport, in part because the net rose up to five feet (1.5 m) above the court. Players hit soft, arching forehands from the baseline until somebody made an error. Rushing up to the net, hitting overhead smashes, and booming forehands were contrary to good tennis manners. Even as tennis became more competitive as the court and net configuration progressed to that seen today, the back-and-forth play was still snail paced by contemporary standards. Those who visit the International Tennis Hall of Fame in Newport, Rhode Island, can watch videos of tennis competitions—the men in long white pants and the women in full, ankle-length skirts—from the first part of the 20th century.

Yet as early at 1913, Wimbledon winner Maurice McLoughlin, known as the California Comet, foreshadowed the future of power tennis with his driving forehands struck from an open stance. In the 1940s Jack Kramer competed with what people called "the big game," hitting hard and rushing to the net. Why did Kramer play with such aggression?

> I play that way because it is the best method for winning. Notre Dame, Michigan, and the Chicago Bears win football games because they go out to score. All champions believe in the adage that a good offense is the best defense. [6]

The aggressive player used a serve-and-volley style that dominated tennis until the latter part of the 20th century. That success was due largely to the greater angle in which a player could hit safely when cutting off an opponent's return by standing closer to the net. But by the late 1900s the development of lighter, larger rackets permitted greater topspin and power that are typical of today's game. In its wake, the serve-and-volley specialists essentially disappeared. In images of the grass courts at Wimbledon taken in 1975, all of the brown wear is in the forecourt. In images taken in 2008, all of the wear is at the baseline.

Illustrating this trend, author and tennis player David Foster Wallace noted that "when Lleyton Hewitt defeated David Nalbandian in the 2002 Wimbledon men's final, there was not a single serve-and-volley point."[9] Wallace also pointed out that one cannot really appreciate the incredible speed of today's tennis when watching a television match:

> You, the viewer, are above and looking down from behind the court. This perspective, as any art student will tell you, 'foreshortens' the court. Real tennis, after all, is three-dimensional, but a TV screen's image is only 2-D. The dimension that's lost (or rather distorted) on the screen is the real court's length, the seventy-eight feet between baselines; and the speed with which the ball traverses this length is a shot's pace, which on TV is obscured, and in person is fearsome to behold.[9]

It would be easy to ascribe the development of today's power game of tennis to the advent of modern racket frames and strings, the astounding improvement in player skill, and the increasing dedication of today's elite competitors to physical fitness. One also might consider that the evolution of tennis into a game of power and speed reflects what goes on in the social culture in which the game is played. Certainly, similar increases in speed, strength, and skill have occurred in other sports, such as basketball and American football. We also witness such increases in daily life, as described in James Gleick's fascinating book *Faster: The Acceleration of Just About Everything*. In today's society, life—from switching TV channels to the impatience of waiting 20 seconds for an elevator—proceeds at high speed.[3] Changes in the game of tennis have mirrored the changes in society.

Popularization of Tennis

Throughout most of its history the game of tennis has been cloaked in an aura of elitism. It began with religious personages and spread to nobles and kings, followed by the leisure class of Victorian England and then a handful of extraordinarily skilled international competitors. No wonder, then, that the common man and woman were not captured by the idea of taking up the game. Tennis was for the country club set: expensive and exclusive.

All that changed. Television brought the excitement of Chris Evert, Pete Sampras, John McEnroe, and Maria Navratilova into everyone's living rooms. Tennis rackets were transformed into lightweight, forgiving instruments that even newcomers to the game could master. Soon everybody seemed to be playing tennis. It was hard to get on a public court, and the number of private clubs grew rapidly.

But like many fads, the energy and interest didn't last forever. In the 1990s the number of players in the United States suddenly dropped, leaving club owners and equipment companies in a lurch. Why? Some think that between the increasing competition for leisure time and the glut of televised sports—golf, football, basketball, extreme sports, and so on—there was too much to choose from. Others cited growing boredom with watching televised tennis matches and their stars, who were losing charisma. Still others thought that people were discovering that playing tennis was not as simple as they had thought or that the cost of new rackets was too high.

In the early 2000s, tennis started to grow again. In the United States this resurgence occurred mainly due to the revitalized efforts of the United States Tennis Association, particularly its emphasis on creating early-development programs for youths. Their numbers indicate that between 2003 and 2008 the number of players in the United States increased by 25 percent and that more than 30 million players were on the court. At present, the number of people playing tennis in the United States equals the entire population of Canada. The biggest age group is 12- to 17-year-olds, which lends hope for the continued growth of the sport in the future.

The popularity of tennis has waxed and waned in other nations as well. These periods have typically followed the successes of native tennis heroes. In Belgium, the courts were filled when Justine Henin and Kim Clijsters were at the top of the women's game. The same thing occurred in Germany from the mid-1980s to the mid-1990s with the successes of Boris Becker and Steffi Graf. China is currently experiencing a tennis boom as the nation follows the success of Li Na. A reported 125 million Chinese fans watched when Li won the 2011 French Open.

Tennis development has faced particular challenges in poor countries such as India, where it is estimated that the majority of the population earns less than $2 daily. Little money is available for the construction of public courts, not to mention lessons or training at private clubs. Still, enthusiasm for tennis has been growing on the subcontinent thanks to the adulation of its tennis stars, first Vijay and Anand Amritraj and more recently the doubles team of Mahesh Bhupathi and Leander Paes.

Throughout the world today, most cultures are obsessed with sport. No doubt much of the current popularity of tennis —among either those who follow international matches daily on the Tennis Channel or those who head out once a month for a set on the high school courts—is included in that enthusiasm. Once again, the evolution of the game of tennis is a reflection of the social culture in which it is played and watched, just as it was on those Sunday afternoons on the lawns of British nobility.

Contributors to Technological Advances

Steady improvements in racket design, court surfaces, balls, shoes, and everything else in tennis have been essential to the development of the game. These technological advances are discussed in chapter 7. In addition, some very influential inventors changed the world of tennis—consciously or not.

- **Edwin Beard Budding.** Social lawn tennis—and all the tennis that came after it in England—would never have been possible if Edwin Beard Budding had not invented the lawn mower in 1830 in Stroud, Gloucestershire. Without lawn mowers, we would still be using grazing animals and sickles to prepare grass courts for competition. Budding, who reportedly had no interest in tennis, conceived the idea for the lawn mower after he observed a bladed cutting machine during a visit to a cloth factory. Most early lawn mowers were pulled by horses, which wore special boots to prevent them from damaging the lawn. Players of tennis, soccer, lacrosse, field hockey, rugby, football, cricket, golf, and croquet are forever in Budding's debt.

- **Charles Goodyear.** An important historical event in 1839 paved the way for tennis to move from the indoor confines of French monasteries to the now-manicured lawns of England. The heavy, solid balls of "real tennis" did not bounce outdoors, and the rubber ball was not an option because in cold weather it became brittle and shattered and in warmer climates it would simply melt. Charles Goodyear, who had just been released from prison in Connecticut after serving time for debt, was working on means of turning raw rubber into a commercially-viable product. One day he accidentally spilled some rubber mixed with sulfur on a hot stove; he found that this rubber was both strong and resistant to temperature. He discovered the process of vulcanization, thus permitting the development of automobile tires. In its wake, the modern tennis ball had arrived.

- **Howard Head.** In 1984 a lightweight, oversized racket that promised more power and control took the tennis world by storm. The story began when Howard Head retired from a lucrative career spent developing aluminum skis. What was Mr. Head going to do with all of his newfound spare time? What else but take up tennis? After $5,000 worth of lessons, however, he remained no more than a mediocre player. But this former aircraft engineer had an idea. Considering that a racket twists less when a ball is struck off center if it has a larger face, he constructed a racket with a 50 percent greater hitting surface area. He bought a ball machine and found that the sweet spot on his new racket was more than four times larger than that on conventional-size rackets. His racket infused fresh hope into millions of otherwise deteriorating recreational players (including Howard Head himself, who became, they say, a respectable club competitor).

None of these inventors were professional tennis players, and you won't see any tennis stadiums bearing their names. But just as much as Sampras, Court, Connors, and King, they were crucial to the development of today's game.

CHAPTER 2

Court Lessons for Life

Racket sports are among the very few individual sports in which one confronts the adversary—face-to-face—in a duel of who can outsmart and outhit whom. Other sports, such as boxing and wrestling, permit bashing the opponent unconscious or pinning him forcefully to a mat. Under normal circumstances, such actions are not permitted on the tennis court. Instead, the tennis competitor must demonstrate patience, self-control, and a mastery of both success and failure and must deal with uncertainty, create a successful playing style, and learn from mistakes. Does this sound a bit like life itself? The game of tennis mimics what goes on in daily existence. This chapter explores how we can learn more about one from the other.

Certainty and Uncertainty

The player stepping onto the court faces a fascinating muddle of predictability. Some things are certain: The rules are straightforward and inflexible, the laws of physics dictate just how the ball will fly, and the players must stay inside the lines. But then the ball crosses the net. At that moment, everything is unpredictable and the opportunity for complete disorder exists—when the player strikes the ball, it can go almost anywhere. The player's job is to use the energy and wisdom of a finely tuned neuromuscular system to bring order to this potential chaos, organize the flight of the ball, and direct the ball back at the waiting opponent. At a fundamental level, tennis is a contest between two players to determine who can best create order out of randomness. A host of other factors play into the unpredictability of tennis: the weather, the skill of the opponent, what the player had for lunch, and what kind of day the player has had. Uncertainty layered on certainty. That's the duality of tennis.

It may be this uncertainty that attracts us to the game. Researchers have looked into why ordinary people play tennis, and many have concluded that factors such as increasing playing skill, maintaining physical fitness and good health, and social benefits. Other more profound explanations—the joy of muscular motion, the satisfaction of trying hard, and the excitement of taking on a physical and mental challenge—have been offered. However, I propose that a primary driving force that causes players to step onto the court is uncertainty itself. In a game with clearly defined rules and the constraints of the physical laws of motion, this unpredictability gives us our grandest pleasures as well as our greatest frustrations. It's why we play. Would you want to play a tennis match in which the outcome was already known and you could predict exactly how you would play? No. The excitement of *not* knowing these things draws us to the game.

Conditions of doubt increase the arousal of the central nervous system. We're energized by the increased action of the sympathetic nervous system and elevated levels of adrenaline circulating in the blood stream. A psychologist would interject here that this attraction to uncertainty is highly pleasurable—and very addictive. We crave more. It's the same reason why people are drawn to roller coasters, can't wait for the next horror movie, or take on the triple-diamond slopes.

Researchers examining the role of uncertainty in our attraction to sports such as tennis have used spectator attendance as their model at athletic events of varying levels of predictability. The research finds that a competition in which the two players are of similar ability, such as Wimbledon, draws more fans than a competition in which one player is clearly superior to the other because the outcome of the latter is more certain. The spectator is considered to be a vicarious participant in the match who experiences arousal by proxy.

Now think about what goes on in daily life, where human behavior is tightly constrained by very rigid biological, legal, and cultural rules. We must eat and drink at regular intervals, and to survive we need to protect ourselves against environmental extremes. We cannot rob liquor stores, run red lights, or cheat on our income tax returns without risking retribution. We are expected to be kind, honest, and loyal. Like in tennis, we must stay inside the lines.

However, layered onto this rigid behavioral structure is uncertainty, which provides the greatest joys and greatest sorrows in life. You're laid off when your company of 40 years suddenly downsizes. You're caught in an afternoon downpour without an umbrella. That chronic cough you thought was allergies turns out to be something more serious. Or, the dentist calls to say he has to cancel your appointment, your favorite football team upsets a hated opponent, and your spouse surprises you with a candle-lit dinner. When you wake in the morning, the events about to unfold that day are a mystery. Although we are often uncomfortable with uncertainty, we must recognize that it provides the friction that drives human existence. Without it, life would be pretty barren. Uncertainty layered on certainty. We confront this duality upon stepping on the tennis court and in the course of daily life.

On-Court Personality

Most tennis players would agree that a player's personality dictates the style of play on the court.[4] Aggressive people tend to play an aggressive game of tennis. The guy who sits at the baseline and is content to simply deliver back every shot hit to him, with a lob here and there, most likely has a shy temperament. The player who is a poaching menace at the net, fires overhead smashes, chases down every ball, and smokes forehands from all corners of the court likely has a large personality that can be intimidating and dominating. This section examines the intriguing question of just *why* and *how* one should adopt a certain playing personality.

First, we must recognize that not much documented scientific evidence backs up the assumption that on-court and off-court behaviors are linked. The closest that I could find was a study performed at the University of Essex in the United

Kingdom. They found that among international elite equestrians, the personalities of the riders (e.g., neuroticism, extroversion, openness, agreeableness) generally matched those of their horses. Whether any link exists between performing horses and behavior on the tennis court is left to the reader's discretion. However, this study does raise some interesting questions:

- Is one on-court behavior better than another?
- Should a player work to alter natural on-court personality?
- Is aggressiveness, both on and off the court, a biologically inherent trait, or is it a product of a cultural environment that fosters pent-up frustration and hostility?
- Can playing competitive tennis *make* a player more aggressive in daily life?

The answers aren't clear, but let's consider the questions for a bit.

The style of tennis that one plays can be seen as consistent with how one faces challenges, whether from an opponent with a backhand slice that is tough to deal with or from a difficult boss. At one end of the spectrum are those who play a steady, controlled game that focuses on the *now*. These players pay attention to each shot and stay within themselves rather than think about the other player. At a 3.5 club level, this is the player who is most consistent, makes the fewest unforced errors, and wins the match. At the other end of the spectrum are players who tell themselves to simply stay relaxed and go for it. They believe that nothing in life, including tennis, needs to be taken seriously. They don't pass judgment on themselves. Rather, they go big, and if their overhead smash ends up in the parking lot, no problem; they just go on to the next point.

Similarly, in daily life we each have a style—for example, conservatism or, conversely, a sense of individual liberty—that is expressed in our personalities.[1] This raises the question of whether we have the freedom to choose how we play or live. The defensive player who is always playing it safe probably knows deep down that a more aggressive approach at certain times would help his game, and vice versa for the aggressive player who realizes that she is overhitting 50 percent of her shots. If she could just calm down and play a more consistent game, she'd move up the ladder.

So why can't we just choose to do those things? Can we assume that we have the freedom to adopt certain behaviors and personality traits? Or are we stuck with what we have? Through the centuries, scientists and philosophers have batted this question around ad nauseam. The answer you get depends on whom you're listening to.

According to the renowned biologist Konrad Lorenz, the tennis player steps on the court with certain aggressive animal instincts, such as competing for food and attracting mates, that are left over from earlier evolutionary days. One's aggressive tendencies are fixed, and a player's temperament on the court is an expression of genetic heritage.

Others see on-court behavior as a product of one's cultural surroundings. In this view, aggression on the court is an expression of a hotbed of frustration, and blowing off steam on the court relieves the tensions encountered in daily life. Aggressiveness manifests on the court not only in one's style of play but also as a temper tantrum, the smashing of an expensive racket, or a violent curse. Court behavior is not immutable; players have the opportunity to try to alter their style of play to what works best.

If history's greatest thinkers can't agree on what style "works" best, the average club tennis player certainly can't be expected to figure it out either. In the end, one could conclude that both sides say the same thing about how to conduct life and play on the tennis court: Just do the best you can, and whatever else that happens will happen. They would, however, disagree on how you best accomplish this goal.

It should be noted that, in the tennis competitor, *aggressiveness* refers to a style of play. Under normal circumstances, a player cannot express physical aggression against the opponent (save an occasional overhead smash aimed at the frontal cortex), and failure to keep such emotions under control is likely to be detrimental to performance. Mental control is a key element of success in the game of tennis. Although the linebacker can flatten an unsuspecting quarterback from the blind side, the tennis player has to keep it all in check.

The question of passive versus aggressive tennis depends a lot on who is playing. This conflict of tennis style might apply to 95 percent of the world's players, but players in the upper echelons of the today's game had better mount a controlled aggressive attack with brilliant defense. If not, they'll come under pointed criticism, as has been leveled by the press at some of the world's top players, for being too passive. On the big stage, aggressive play—going for the big shots—is considered equivalent to competitiveness, and the top players can't compete without a well-rounded, highly aggressive game.

Psychologists have done a considerable amount of research that examines the link between personality and performance in athletics. Not surprisingly, these studies show that successful athletes at the highest levels of international play score low in measures of tension, depression, fatigue, and confusion and high in measures of vigor and positive mind-set.[4] Interestingly, however, individuals who are just beginning a sport or who compete at lower levels generally don't demonstrate this same association between personality traits and performance.

Making Decisions

Daily life is filled with a nonending series of decisions. Sometimes these decisions are mundane, such as choosing what to eat for dinner. Other times they're more momentous, such as choosing a spouse or selecting a career. Sometimes they're critically important, such as an airline pilot making decisions during an emergency landing. Psychologists and other behavioral scientists have long been fascinated with just *how* humans make such decisions.

The traditional assumption, which dates back to the ancient Greeks, is that humans, as rational beings, make conscious decisions by gathering information, carefully analyzing the pros and cons, and selecting the optimal choice. However, this often may not be the case. Recent neurological studies have pin-pointed where decision-making functions reside in the brain. The prefrontal cortex at the front of the cerebrum is respon-sible for cognitive decision making when an individual weighs the pluses and minuses in a thoughtful manner. Surprisingly, though, scientists have found that individuals make most deci-sions throughout the day using a different part of the brain: structures directly connected to past experiences and emo-tional motives. It seems that impulsivity and emotions beneath consciousness often hold sway over cognitive decision making.

Parallels exist with how a player makes decisions on the tennis court. One might assume that the brain neatly thinks out choices such as shot selection, striking the ball with the racket, and court movement and that one strategizes according to a rational, cognitive thought process. In other words, that the willful, conscious brain is in control and that the thinking individual makes the choices.

However, in real life this is for the most part not true. Think about it in the context of how one loses a point in tennis. It seems that basically three possibilities exist:

1. The opponent delivers a super, nonreturnable shot, such as an ace, a drop shot, or a cross-court forehand that skims the line.
2. The player makes a tactical error, such as delivering a shot right to the wheel house of an opponent who has a smashing forehand, failing to lob over the doubles team that is crouching over the net, or sticking to the baseline after rendering a high bouncing drive deep to the op-ponent's backhand corner.
3. The player makes an unforced error, such as driving an easy overhead into the net, sending a setup volley long instead of into an open court, or watching a mis-hit fly into the next court over.

Only errors in the second category are true mistakes on the part of the player because they're the only actions over which one has conscious control. The player should have recognized the situation and thought, *That guy has an incredible forehand, and I should avoid giving him the opportunity*. The unforced errors that fall into the third category—the ones that drive people nuts—are not really the fault of the player. Rather, they're mistakes that are not under conscious control.

There's just no time for you to consciously reason this out. For example, imagine that your opponent somehow manages to return your kick second serve and that the ball is crossing the net toward your forehand side. What do you need to do? Run to the right and either forward or backward to get your feet into the best position to strike the ball, keep your eyes on the ball, decide which type of forehand shot to make, change your grip on the racket accordingly, bend your knees, bring your racket back, time the racket swing to correspond with the arrival of the ball, direct the ball with a proper trajectory, and speed into an optimal spot while staying aware of the position of your opponent—all in just a second or two. That's just not enough time to make a cognitive decision; your prefrontal lobe doesn't work that fast. It wouldn't matter if you had a little more time, either, such as while waiting to strike a high lob. The prefrontal cortex just has too many bits of information to process at one time. Therefore, you have to go on automatic and let your subconscious brain return the shot. This part of the brain is very sharp—it has learned from all the practice hours you've put in, the previous matches you've played, and the errors you've made in the past. It puts into motion, without your conscious input, all the actions you have to perform quickly to return the shot.

When players step onto the court, they are actually two players. One is a thinking, conscious player who considers options and makes cognitive decisions and game strategies. Let's call this the thinking player. The other player, in the subconscious mind, has learned the game from past experiences—including mistakes—and works beneath the level of conscious awareness. We'll call this the automatic player. The two complement each other, and both are important for tennis success. However, they can also get in each other's way and keep us from playing our best tennis in critical moments.

Unforced errors are a breakdown in the automatic player, over which one really has no control. That a player just drove a powder-puff second serve into the net doesn't mean she's unintelligent or that she lacks personal worth as a human being. The only decision she could have made to prevent that error would have been to practice more intensely, which is the best way for the automatic player to groove that mechanism for delivering a perfect serve and make it work most consistently.

What happens is that the thinking player gets mad at the automatic player, which is not really fair. Even the automatic player can have a bad day now and then. It would be nice to know how and why this happens. Was it the player's choice of breakfast cereal that day? The weather? The alignment of the stars in the zodiac? Some days the automatic player just can't miss and the tennis player is in a groove. Other days everything is long, wide, or out. It has something to do with just the right greasing of the neuromuscular machinery, which a person can't willfully control.

How should the player respond to the three ways of losing a point?

1. If the opponent makes an incredible shot, applaud the perfect hit.
2. If the player makes a tactical mistake, try refocusing on the game at hand.
3. If the player makes an unforced error, smile and practice more.

The only option that deserves approbation is number two. That's where cognitive decision making on the court—direct from the prefrontal cortex—is the player's responsibility. So, in the end, yes, tennis is a game about decision making, but for the most part those decisions are not under the player's conscious control. The best way to develop good decision-making on the court is to groove the automatic player, so that in critical situations that subconscious player knows what to do.

Accepting Mistakes

People sometimes see tennis as a contest in which two players vie for who can score the most points by delivering winning, nonreturnable shots. No, tennis, like life, is a game of mistakes.[5] Watch a match being played and take note. Almost every point involves an error on the part of one of the players, even when it doesn't seem obvious. For example, the returner leans out wide as the ace serve comes down the T, or the putaway overhead was caused by a lob that didn't quite have enough oomph. In tennis, the goal is to minimize errors. The player who errs the least will probably win the match.

This is true at the elite level as well. It's not rare to see a talented professional player make 40 or 50 unforced errors—the same kinds of mistakes players down at the 3.5 level make, which is reassuring to us all—in a losing match. It's hard to talk about records for unforced errors because the definition may vary from locale to locale. However, one female professional player (name withheld) is said to have racked up 100 unforced errors in a three-set match. And John McEnroe is said to hold the unofficial record for fewest unforced errors in a Grand Slam final: just four at Wimbledon in 1984 against Jimmy Connors.

Is there a way to keep from making errors, both those caused by misguided cognitive thinking or those coming from glitches in the unconscious brain? Searching through tennis magazines, self-help videos, and instructional books, players can find a great deal of advice on the matter, and much of it conflicting: One can reduce errors by striking the ball harder or softer, concentrating or relaxing, practicing more, taking lessons, and so on. This book endorses the advice of physicist Howard Brody, who believes that players can best limit errors by keeping the scientific principles of tennis in mind.[2] These have to do with angles of ball–racket interaction, how hard the ball is hit, spin, and service techniques. The laws of physics as they relate to the game of tennis are not difficult to understand and for most players should prove useful. Chapter 6 examines these in detail.

Legendary player John McEnroe had incredible success at Wimbledon, winning three singles titles there and setting an unofficial record for fewest unforced errors in a Grand Slam final with just four.

PA Archive/Press Association Images

Although basing tennis play on principles of science is sound, these strategies need to be ingrained through practice and repeated play. The brain has no time to figure out physics when a player is streaking toward the net for a backhand volley; the actions have to be automatic. These techniques need to be taught to the automatic player—the one who plays when there's no time to think. That educational process involves trial and error through the experiences gained during repeated practice and play.

The good news is that making errors is actually the best way to improve game play. You can say that you will stop hitting volleys directly to your opponent's forehand—working out cognitive strategies helps. But research has indicated that most decision making during tennis play is performed by the subconscious mechanisms discussed previously. The question is how the automatic player *knows* how to play the game. The answer: It learns by watching you make mistakes.

When you make a perfect shot, the automatic player recognizes how it was achieved and tries to replicate it next time. If the ball flies into the net, it notes that too and says, "What I did last time didn't work. I won't do that again." Each time you make a mistake, your brain cells adjust and new electrical connections are made—all while you are unaware that it is happening. As Jonah Lehrer put it, "Expertise is simply the wisdom that emerges from cellular error. Mistakes aren't things to be discouraged. On the contrary, they should be cultivated and carefully investigated."[7] The lesson for tennis is to keep practicing and to not be so hard on your automatic player. The automatic player learns best from mistakes, so embrace them and know that each one is a part of the path to better tennis.

Withstanding Defeat

Everyone hates to lose. Everyone wants to win the best job, the scholarship application to the best college, and the promotion. When these things don't happen, the horrible feeling pops up that maybe it's not all worth it.

Tennis is without a doubt an unpredictable game, but one thing certain: In any match, precisely 50 percent of the players will win and 50 percent will lose. That's a lot of losing. Defeat is a part of the game. People say that if you don't play you can't win, but they forget to tell you that if you don't play you can't lose either. If you can't stand losing, maybe the 50 percent odds aren't so good.

Losing in tennis seems to be a particularly wretched experience filled with even more angst, anger, and sense of worthlessness than many other setbacks in life. In case there was any question, scientists have spent grant money verifying the emotional distress of defeat. One group of investigators, for example, unabashedly reported that NCAA Division III female athletes who lost a contest were more anxious and frustrated than those who won; the latter described feelings of improved mental well-being and self-esteem.

Researchers have also found that different parts of the brain are involved in feelings of triumph and defeat. A report from the Serby Institute for General and Forensic Psychiatry in Moscow indicated that electrical potentials in the brain increased in the left posterior associative cortex when players of a televised tennis game were victorious and that potentials in the right frontal area decreased when they lost.[6]

Everyone would agree that it's important for players to control their tempers on the court when losing and to display at least a good face of sportsmanship in defeat. But how does one cope? A review of the popular tennis literature provides a long list of suggested strategies and mantras that can be repeated.

- Buck up; it's just a game (naïve)
- Learn from the mistakes (educational)
- Everybody faces defeat, even Roger Federer (observant)
- Relax; being out there competing is what counts (philosophical)
- Go out and indulge in a big hot-fudge sundae (gastronomic)

However, extensive personal experience has shown that none of these are effective. The simple fact is that losing is very painful. Philosophy is fine, but time is the best healer. For most people, the anguish predictably resolves in 12 to 24 hours. The best advice seems to be to just ride it out. That goes for all the bumps in life, too.

Standing Alone

In the spirit of a balanced discussion, it should be noted that researchers Miguel Crespo at the International Tennis Federation in Valencia, Spain, and his Australian colleague Machar Reid have argued that much about tennis separates it from the experiences of normal life.[3] They state, "Tennis has no substitutes, no timeouts, no in-game coaching, and often in tournaments, no second chance. Throughout, players must adapt their games to ever-changing playing conditions (i.e., court surfaces, altitudes, balls, competition systems) and many different opponents." Patrick McEnroe, in his excellent televised tennis commentary, has noted that when a tennis player steps on the court, he is totally alone and stripped of all usual social support structures. All strategies, decisions, response to adversity—everything—are solely on the player's shoulders. As Andy Roddick once stated in a postgame interview, "When the going gets tough, you can't just pass the ball off." A player can learn a lot about himself and maybe gain resilience and self-confidence out on the court alone. In facing the demands of life, of course, one can often just hide in the crowd. But out on that tennis court, all alone, a player can learn a lot about himself and maybe gain in resilience and self-confidence.

CHAPTER 3

Tennis Skill Development

This chapter explores how the human body goes about learning the game of tennis. The bottom line is that at the present time we don't know—and are not even close to knowing—all the answers. But researchers are now beginning to unravel the mysteries of the brain and all the connections that form the basis for learning to play the game. In the end, this information promises to pay dividends for tennis players and their coaches. For resting in the pages that follow are the mechanistic secrets that underlie the amazing "plasticity" of the human body. We learn the game and get better when we practice. But how can this occur?

The brain of an adult human contains about 100 billion nerve cells. These nerve cells, called neurons, are some of the building blocks of the body. Each cell has numerous branches called dendrites. Neurons communicate with other neurons via synapses and send out electrical messages through a single fiber called an axon. Information from the dendrites of one neuron is communicated to the dendrites of its neighbor across the synapse by chemical agents called neurotransmitters.

More astounding and incomprehensible than the sheer quantity of these neurons is the way these cells connect with each other, form networks, and arrange themselves to serve the brain's myriad functions. Try to picture billions of dendrites enmeshed together and electrical signals flashing across synapse spaces, communicating, organizing, and directing. We're just not capable of appreciating the complexity of the functioning of the central nervous system.

The brain provides the electrical hookups that cause muscles to move about. On the tennis court, the brain orchestrates this motor activity by firing a finely tuned cascade of contractions that enable us to run, chase down lobs, and deliver scorching cross-court backhands. All of these activities are performed automatically by a gelatinous mass the size of a small lunch pail. The brain operates 24 hours a day, 7 days a week, for about 85 years without stopping. Think about it.

Humans have mechanisms that are able to trigger an increased capacity for physical performance through practice. Physiologists have traditionally explained this adaptation—this plasticity—by the augmented activity of specific genes in inherited chromosomal material that are responsible for enhancing body functions. These genes are stimulated by repetitive bodily activity (i.e., training), and they react by sending out directives that enhance the physical, biochemical, or physiological processes responsible for the performance of that particular activity. (The story is more complex, however, because other regulatory agents control which genes are turned on. This process is discussed further chapter 4.) The processes of physical training, gene response, and adaptive changes in the central nervous system improve tennis skill.

In light of the ability of the body and brain to adapt with practice, some intriguing questions are important to understanding how to improve one's own tennis skills, how to introduce young players to the game, and the most effective methods for teaching the sport.

- Why does tennis performance improve when people are placed in a training program?
- What physical and physiological changes create the change in tennis performance?
- In identical training programs, will all people improve to the same extent and at the same rate? If not, what factors determine who gets better and who doesn't?
- Where do the future elite players come from in this mass of students? Is their success a matter of inherited characteristics (nature) or the volume and quality of training (nurture)?

- Will younger people improve faster than older people? Is training most effective at a certain age?
- Is one method for teaching tennis more effective than another?

Much discussion and controversy has swirled around these questions, and there is no lack of (sometimes passionate) opinions. Much uncertainty remains, particularly regarding how research data might be applied to the real world of play on the tennis court. Because these questions are of vital interest to physicians, coaches, and athletes, a good deal of research attention has been focused on providing useful answers. Much research in motor learning has utilized studies involving simple motor tasks, such as speed of finger tapping, conducted in tightly controlled laboratory conditions. An increased understanding of the science behind motor learning—particularly as aided by new brain-imaging technologies—is beginning to provide some ideas that might be of practical value in stepping up one's game.

The Adapting Body

Plasticity, which is the ability to alter structure and function in response to environmental stimuli, is a defining characteristic of the human organism. Sufficient repetition of a bodily function—be it physical, physiological, or mental—enhances one's ability to perform that activity. Quite remarkably, this capacity for self-improvement is observed in all domains of human endeavor. A person who lifts weights for a couple months will get stronger, one who runs three miles (4.8 km) three times a week will be able to go farther, and one who practices the clarinet every night will soon be playing Brahms. Regular repetition can help a person memorize poems, understand how to play chess, acquire a new language, and learn to play tennis. Keep repeating that backhand slice and it will improve.

What's striking is that all the various functions that improve with training or practice occur through very different physiological and physical means. With tennis training, a player improves stroke technique (a neuromuscular adaptation), becomes stronger (via increased protein content in the muscle), and can more easily endure third-set tie breaks (via expansion of the cardiovascular system and increased density of mitochondria for energy utilization in the skeletal muscle). In the brain, changes in the neurons and their connections permit a player to track and meet the ball with greater facility and react more quickly at the net. All of these adaptations that improve one's tennis game occur through mechanisms that are totally separate.

All humans have plasticity with training, but the extent of plasticity varies from person to person and the degree of adaptation depends on numerous factors, including the specificity, timing, and intensity of training. The downside of plasticity with training is that the improvement observed is apparent only when one performs the exact activity used during training. For example, if a player lifts weights for six weeks to improve arm strength, she will get stronger only in motions of the arm that mimic those used during training. The lesson is to be sure you're using proper technique before you strike 200 forehands from the ball machine. Otherwise, you'll be wasting your time and cementing an improper stroke motion.

To be effective, practice needs to be sufficiently intense and progressive. (Chapter 4 discusses deliberate practice in detail.) Athletes recognize the importance of timing practice sessions on a weekly or yearly basis (so-called periodization of training) and the need for sufficient rest between practice sessions. The rate at which training stress increases is critical. The common error of doing too much too soon leads to injury or reduction in performance (i.e., burnout).

For training to be effective, the athlete must have adequate time for recovery and adaptation. A common misconception is that improvements occur during training. True, improvement in repetitive actions such as finger motions may occur, but for most skills the exercise stimulus is a stressor. One's ability to perform an activity is enhanced as the body responds to the stress with mechanisms that improve that function. When a person lifts weights, the stress on the muscles stimulates responses that augment protein synthesis in the muscle cells, which increases strength. When one pounds out five miles (8 km) in a training run, the adaptations increase muscle oxidative capacity and enlarge the size of the heart's ventricles. It takes time—during rest—for this to occur.

Is it better to practice at a particular time of day? Maybe. Tennis performance, like other motor activities, may follow a circadian pattern that ranges over a 24-hour period. In one study, the serve velocity of tennis players was faster at 6:00 p.m. than at 9:00 a.m. Unfortunately, the opposite was observed for service accuracy, which was superior in the morning. Although this report does suggest that a player's tennis performance might vary with time of day, no research data point to the time of day when training in most effective. A few reports have indicated that training in the afternoon optimizes improvements in both aerobic fitness and muscle strength. Clearly, more information is needed here.

In summary, human bodies do improve with tennis training, which involves alterations in the many facets that contribute to performance on the court. However, to optimize such adaptations one must pay close attention to how and when such training should occur. Researchers are just beginning to understand the factors that influence this training effect.

Motor Learning Process

Just how do we learn—and improve—new motor functions? The story of a pair of Midwestern investigators who were interested in the skill of telegraphers set the stage for insights into the answer to this question

On a cold Indiana afternoon in 1899, Professor William Lowe Bryan and his colleague, Superintendent Noble Harter, sat in a university office with piles of data in front of them. They had just completed a study that examined individuals' rates of learning in the sending and receiving of Morse code signals by telegraph. The numbers showed that at least two years of regular practice was required before the participants reached a high level of expertise in this neuromuscular task. Their attention, however, was drawn to a second finding. The curve they plotted for participants' skill improvement in receiving messages increased with time over the first few months, then plateaued briefly, then increased again. They were told, too, that the experience during training of expert telegraphers was that this early rapid improvement was often followed by a second plateau and subsequent increase.[3]

The explanation for this pattern was not at all clear, so the two investigators were free to hypothesize. They suggested that participants learned how to receive messages in Morse code in stages—attention to letters, then words, then sentences—and that the rapid ascents of performance represented the learning phase of each stage. The plateau, they conjectured, might be a period during which that particular phase of the skill was on automatic and no active learning occurred.

The ability of humans to learn and improve performance of neuromuscular and mental tasks with practice has been recognized since antiquity. However, this study was among the first to begin to decipher the process by which such learning occurs. The authors espoused two principles. First, they stated that the active, attention-focused task becomes automatic with time and requires no conscious focus. Second, they proposed a process called hierarchical learning, in which acquisition of motor skills occurs in stages. The participant first achieves simple, elemental aspects of the task, which then provide a basis for more complex learning.

Contemporary motor learning experts have designated the initial phase of training as a period of explicit, or cognitive, learning. During this phase one is introduced to a new task, the performance of which demands conscious attention. In the first week of tennis class, a student must bring her mind to the task: Run to the ball, keep the racket back, bend the knees, move body weight forward during the swing, watch the ball, keep the wrist firm with the proper grip, sweep upward during the swing, follow through. It's a clunky way to learn a new motor task, but it works, particularly if the learner focuses on one element at a time. The learner can achieve improvement quite rapidly with such repeated, purposeful movement, but, ultimately, the upward curve is limited. Because real success in tennis play does not allow time for such conscious contemplation of every return and shot, motor skills must be integrated even further.

With continued practice the body moves on to implicit learning, in which conscious effort is released and the player performs the actions of playing tennis automatically without thinking. In that stage, the automatic player (discussed in chapter 2), who is in the subconscious depths of the central nervous system, is learning the game. The objective is to ingrain stroke technique, visual tracking, body control, visuomotor coincident timing, and court sense into the subconscious brain. Eventually, most of the game is turned over to this skilled controller, leaving the player time to strategize or analyze the opponent's weakness.

Just how does the automatic player learn to play the game? Those in charge of training fighter pilots and gunners may have they answer. They've utilized a process from the realms of engineering and computer science that says that motor learning during physical training occurs through the detection and self-correction of errors. In this process, the brain carefully monitors performance, detects deviations from proper actions, and automatically makes functional adjustments that correct the errors. On the tennis court, the automatic player does the same thing. The details of how it accomplishes this are still fuzzy, but the process involves changing electrical connections in the brain and its pathways.

A number of recent brain-imaging studies have indicated that this shift from purposeful cognitive attention to automatic, subconscious-directed play may be reflected in shifts in the regions of the brain that control motor function. For example, A. Floyer-Lea and P.M. Matthews at the Centre for Functional Magnetic Resonance Imaging of the Brain at the University of Oxford used functional magnetic resonance imaging (MRI) to examine changes in participants' brains in response to learning a visuomotor skill (i.e., tracking a moving target by pressing on

Elite players like Italy's Sara Errani, shown hitting a backhand during the women's singles final at the Mexican Open Tennis Tournament in 2013, have performed so much continued practice that they're able to perform an action without thinking, leaving more time to analyze strategy.

Pedro Mera/Photoshot/Icon SMI

a pressure plate).[7] Functional MRI noninvasively estimates blood flow to areas of the brain as a surrogate marker of level of neurological activity. It provides information on the collective neurologic activity in certain regions of the brain rather than the electrical activity in individual neurons. Using this technique, the degree of neurological function and the anatomical areas associated with particular motor functions can be identified. For example, if a person takes a whiff of an onion, the areas of the brain associated with smell light up.

Floyer-Lea and Matthews observed two distinct temporal-related patterns of brain activity. Initially, during the attention-demanding stage, activity was widely distributed in several cortical regions (prefrontal, bilateral sensorimotor, and parietal) associated with cognitive decision making. As learning progressed and performance improved, this pattern was replaced by increased activity in subcortical motor regions (particularly the cerebellar dentate, thalamus, and putamen) associated with subconscious brain function. The authors concluded that this shift occurred as the task became more automatic. If this is true, they and others have demonstrated that the hierarchical model of psychomotor learning envisaged by Bryan and Harter in telegraph operators has parallels—a shift in control centers with increasing performance automaticity—in the central nervous system.

This explicit–implicit model also bears importance in understanding and optimizing techniques for tennis teaching. In explicit teaching, the coach verbally points out the skill to be accomplished by the student and then offers positive or negative feedback and specific instruction. The information is in the player's consciousness, and she can think about and cognitively attempt to respond to the coach's guidance. For example, the coach asks the player to focus on the way her opponent slices down on a backhand shot, explaining that this causes the ball to skid low on her side of the court. After a couple times seeing this visual clue, the player will be able to consciously see a slice backhand coming.

In implicit teaching, on the other hand, the coach says nothing. The player simply watches his opponent slice 10 backhands and observes how the ball lands on his side of the net. He then unconsciously adjusts his stroke to meet the skidding ball.

Which is more effective for teaching the game: providing verbal directives to a thinking student or letting experience teach lessons on a subconscious level? Studies have compared the success of the two approaches in teaching skills such as anticipating service returns. The results have generally been conflicting and provide no obvious conclusions. However, such investigations suggest that those who learn by implicit processes are more likely perform better in stressful situations (i.e., actual competitions).

Michael Reid, a prominent tennis researcher at the University of Western Australia, commented, "This debate may be somewhat mediated if implicit and explicit learning are not viewed as dichotomous states of knowledge but rather the end points on a continuum."[17] That is, you need both. Reid emphasizes that supplying informed, directed information to the student is important but that implicit self-discovery approaches emphasize coaches as facilitators rather than dictators of the learning process. Teaching by implicit learning does not mean that the coach has the hour off. The coach must identify the key skills important for training focus and provide feedback to direct students into the proper learning drills. Too, he needs to provide guidance in developing match-based problem solving and skills for enhancing real-world performance in competition. Because everyone learns differently, the progress of certain students is likely to be facilitated by one approach over the other.

Skill Acquisition

Jonah Lehrer wrote, "The most mysterious thing about the human brain is that the more we know about it, the deeper our own mystery becomes."[15] Nowhere is this more evident than in the search for identifying the neurophysiological underpinnings of the mechanisms for improving performance through tennis training. A good number of anatomical, physiological, and biochemical adaptations have been described at all levels of the central and peripheral nervous systems, but no coherent single model has emerged. It is likely that an enhanced top-spin forehand developed after many practice hours on the court reflects a combination of such responses.

The training effect has typically been described in vague terms, such as "grooving" a particular neuromuscular functional pathway or "acquiring muscle memory."[19] Researchers have long sought a more precise explanation of just how the body accomplishes these adaptations.[8] This section provides a quick review of the possible mechanisms responsible for motor learning that underlie learning the game of tennis. Some of these are better documented experimentally than others, and it should be noted that few, if any, have been examined in athletes.

Hebb's Law

In the 1940s, neurophysiological adaptations in response to motor or mental training were considered to reflect increases in communication between neurons. According to Hebb's law, named for the Canadian neurophysiologist who proposed it, "When an axon of cell A is near enough to excite cell B and repeatedly or persistently take part in firing it, some growth process or metabolic change takes place in one or both cells such that A's efficiency, as one of the cells firing B, is increased."[10]

Animal Studies on Synapses

Studies in animals, mostly rats, have supported the concept that training changes the firing pattern of neural tissues and increases the amplitude of cellular electrical potentials. With physical training, new synapses may be created or previous existing lateral connections may be unmasked. Increases in length and branching of dendrites have also been observed in rodents after a period of physical training.

Jeffrey Kleim and colleagues in the department of psychology at the University of Illinois trained rats to run an obstacle course consisting of rotating cylinders, dowel rods, a suspended chain, and wooden blocks.[13] Histological examination afterward revealed that the trained rats showed an overall greater increase in number of synapses per neuron compared with control animals.

Human Studies on Synapses

Research data on physiological responses to athletic training are scant. However, the information that is available is consistent with findings regarding cerebral responses to training in animals and musicians. Ladina Bezzola and colleagues at the International Normal Aging and Plasticity Imaging Center at the University of Zurich examined changes in MRI after exposing 40- to 60-year-old participants to 40 hours of nonstructured golf training.[2] Compared with nontrained controls, the trained participants showed significant (2-4 percent) increases in gray matter content in brain areas associated with motor learning (primary somatosensory cortex, inferior frontal gyrus, and inferior parietal lobule. The researchers also found a strong direct association between the magnitude of this increase in the parietal-occipital junction and the intensity of the training. Similarly, a cross-sectional study by Lutz Jancke at the University of Zurich found that elite golfers had greater volume of gray matter in regions of the brain responsible for motor activity than nonelite golfers (e.g., the frontoparietal networks including premotor and parietal areas).[12]

Exercise scientist A.J. Pearce and colleagues at the University of Western Australia studied a group of five elite badminton players.[16] They found that, compared with nonathletes, the athletes had greater electrical stability and changes in topography in regions of the cerebral cortex related to control of the playing hand.

It should be noted that while the above studies reveal certain regional changes in the brain with training or physical expertise, the actual adaptations or physiological changes in these areas remains unclear. The data do support, however, the concept that changes within the brain contribute to functional improvements that are predictably observed with sports training.

Taken collectively, the evidence is both consistent and compelling that sport training can enhance the size and function of pertinent motor areas in the gray matter of the brain. Information specific to tennis is lacking, but little doubt exists that adaptations in the cerebral cortex that result from practice time on the courts are instrumental in improving performance. What happens on microscopic and biochemical levels as the brain adapts with practice is not clear, but based on animal studies one could reasonably infer that responses involving improved synaptic connections and function play a key role.

Human Studies on Adaptations in Cortical Gray Matter

Insights into training-stimulated brain alterations in human beings were rather restricted until the advent of noninvasive brain-imaging methodologies that have been developed over the past several decades. Functional MRI, positron emission topography, transcranial magnetic stimulation (in which magnet-induced electrical current is used to stimulate brain centers), and fractional anisotropy (used to assess integrity of brain white matter) have all been used to assess brain activity.[8,20] These techniques have permitted a new understanding of both anatomical and functional responses to physical and mental training. It is now possible to visualize changes in the brain while people are training. These imaging techniques reveal shifting of anatomical sites that control motor activity as well as increases in size, density, and function of these brain centers. It is still not possible to see what's going on at microstructural or biochemical levels, but such regional adaptations in cortical gray matter have generally been considered to reflect the number of neurons firing or the increasing efficacy of the synapses that connect them.

Human studies of adaptations underlying neural plasticity to training have largely involved professional musicians. In cross-sectional studies (i.e., studies that simply compare imaging findings in musicians and nonmusicians), certain areas —the corpus callosum (where nerve wires connect the two cerebral hemispheres), auditory areas, regions specializing in visuospatial skills, and motor areas that control the motion of the hand on the instrument—are observed to be more prominent in trained participants. Some studies show that the extent of changes in the brain is greater in individuals who started practicing at an early and in those who display a higher level of musical skill. According to Lutz Jancke, among these cross-sectional human studies, "There is considerable evidence that highly proficient subjects demonstrate specific neuro-anatomical features in brain areas involved in the control of the particular task for which the subjects demonstrate their particular expertise."[12]

Better evidence for the contribution of cortical alterations to motor plasticity comes from studies that measured brain changes over the actual time course of training. Such longitudinal studies are few but still support this influence. For example, neuropsychologist Bogdan Draganski and colleagues at the University of Lausanne obtained MRI images in individuals before and after a three-month period of juggling practice.[5] These images indicated that gray matter density in brain areas that are important for juggling (intraparietal sulcus and the human movement territory) increased with training. However, a repeat MRI scan performed three months after juggling practice ended showed that the brain areas in question had reverted ~~back~~ to their pretraining dimensions. Moreover, the participants had lost all juggling skills. According to Lutz Jancke, you have to "use it or lose it."[12]

This may apply to something undertaken in the short term, such as three months of juggling. But according to Leslie Ungerleider and colleagues at the National Institutes of Health in the United States, if a motor skill is overlearned (i.e., learned to the point that it becomes automatic), then "the skilled behavior is thought to become resistant to both interference and the simple passage of time. Once overlearned, a motor skill can thus be readily retrieved with reasonable performance despite long periods without practice."[21] For example, people seldom forget how to ride a bicycle.

New Neuron Growth

A while back, everyone in the science world accepted as fact that the brain is able to create new neurons for only a short period early in life. After normal child development was complete, the process was finished and the brain couldn't make any more. However, biologists have proven this idea wrong.

As early as the late 1960s, it was suggested that adult animals—rats, cats, and guinea pigs—are capable of forming new neurons, and the validity of this phenomenon is now well established. Primates such as marmosets and macaques form new neurons throughout the life span. Researchers have observed that these cells form mainly in the hippocampus of the brain, a region that is critical for learning and memory. Also, this process might facilitate the acquisition of new skills, motor or otherwise. When birds learn to sing, they use new brain cells.

Henriette van Praag at the National Institutes of Health and other researchers have demonstrated that regular physical activity stimulates the creation of new neurons in animals.[22] When a rodent participates in a program of regular wheel running, the number and life span of new neurons in its hippocampus increases by a factor of three to four. These investigators have also shown in mice that exercise reduces the rate of decline in the formation of new neurons that normally occurs with aging or pregnancy.

This information is very exciting for those who feel that exercise can play an important role in improving cognitive function of individuals with dementia or other forms of mental illness. Viewed from another angle, it is not unreasonable to suggest that neurogenesis (i.e., the increased formation of new neurons) with regular exercise might play a role in the plasticity of neuromuscular function found in sport training.

Some, however, remain skeptical. Professor R. Douglas Fields at the National Institutes of Health notes, "Neurogenesis provides relatively few cells, and some changes seen using MRI are evident more rapidly than could be accounted for the by generation of new neurons."[6]

The idea that growth of new neurons could play a role in improvements of physical skill—including tennis—is intriguing. Clearly, however, there is a great deal more to be learned regarding the role of neurogenesis in plasticity of human performance.

Changes in Brain Chemistry

Neurons in the brain communicate with each other electrically via chemical substances that permit electrical transmissions at the synapses. In animal studies, the amount of certain neurotransmitters in the brain—norepinephrine, dopamine, and serotonin—increases with exercise. Because investigations such as these are prohibitive in humans, the relevance of such findings to an individual trying to improve a tennis game is only speculative. It's not a reach, however, to suggest that chemical changes in the central nervous system could play a role in adaptations that improve performance during tennis training.

Professors Joshua Sanes and Jeff Lichtman of the Center for Brain Science at Harvard University noted that 121 molecules have been suggested to participate in changes in synaptic transmission.[18] The list includes neurotransmitters and neurotrophins (e.g., brain-derived neurotrophic factor, or BDNF, which as well as factors that alter intracellular genetic expression and proteins that influence vesicles and adhesion processes in synapse formation.

A great deal of research attention has focused on BDNF, which increases with exercise and, at least in animals, has positive effects on learning and memory. If BDNF is injected into the hippocampus of a rat brain, the animal will exhibit increased long-term task memory. Research recognizes that BDNF stimulates synapse development and plasticity as well as neuronal connectivity.

Levels of BDNF can be measured in human blood, and some research suggests that such concentrations reflect brain BDNF content. An acute bout of intense aerobic exercise causes an increase in blood levels of BDNF, but whether this reflects a true increase in BDNF concentrations in the brain is uncertain. Polish researchers Jerzy Zoladz and A. Pilc have commented that such a conclusion "should be considered with caution, since the contribution from other peripheral sources of BDNF release during exercise, such as the platelets, vascular endothelial cells, smooth muscle cells and other cells, requires more research."[23]

These same authors also showed that a period of endurance training increases blood levels of BDNF in humans, which would nicely support the idea that this agent has a role in improving motivation, arousal, and physical capacities during the training process. Unfortunately, other studies have found no such BDNF responses to physical training. In a review of experimental investigations, Kristel Knaepen and colleagues in the department of human physiology and sports medicine at Vrije Universiteit in Brussels found that only two of six studies described a significantly higher BDNF response to a bout of acute exercise after participants engaged in an aerobic or strength-training program.[14]

The role of biochemical responses in the brain, by enhancing electrical transmissions, in training adaptations in athletes remains a tantalizing but unproven proposition. As noted previously, improvements in mental state (e.g., motivation, self-confidence, and arousal) might be a route through which such chemical changes could influence sport training and performance. Such changes would bear significant importance to the game of tennis, with its reliance on both mental and physical factors.

Adaptations in White Matter and Myelin Formation

The discussion in this chapter has focused almost entirely—as traditionally has been the case—on the gray matter of the brain. This mantle is where neurons reside, where electrical transmissions originate, and where synapses communicate. The data presented so far in this discussion indicate that alterations in structure and function of the gray matter are key factors in adaptations to motor learning. However, recent information suggests that the white matter of the brain—often ignored in these investigations—may also play an instrumental role in improvements in motor function with training. Specifically, it has been proposed that improved performance could reflect increased formation of myelin, the white substance that forms the lining, or insulation, of axons.

The white matter, which constitutes one half of the human brain, comprises the axons that extend from the neurons that reside in the gray matter. Its white color comes from the myelin that coats these axons. This insulation, which is manufactured by cells called oligodendrocytes, is important for electrical transmission. Normally, myelin accumulates along axons during fetal life and childhood and is felt to be instrumental in the development of normal learning and motor milestones during the growing years. Some propose that the repeated nerve traffic involved in motor training might thicken myelin coats and enhance neural transmission—and, consequently, neuromuscular function.

The idea that white matter might play a role in physical training originates from an animal study in which some rats were raised in an "enriched environment"—with lots of friends and toys to play with—and others were kept in impoverished surroundings. At autopsy, the animals in the former group showed a greater expansion of white matter, including more pronounced development of myelin. Evidence in mice, too, suggests that repetitive electrical activity along nerve tracts in the central nervous system can stimulate myelin formation.

In humans, white matter function is estimated indirectly using a technique called diffusion tensor imaging, which assesses the direction of water diffusion in tissue (fractional anisotropy, or FA). Changes in this measure are interpreted as revealing white matter integrity because alterations are not specific to myelin production and can reflect axon caliber and organization of fibers (e.g., density, crossing, and branching).

Studies using this technique to assess the potential influence of white matter on training of motor skills in humans have provided conflicting results. Sara Bengtsson and colleagues at the Karolinska Institute in Stockholm compared white matter structure in eight professional concert pianists and nonmusicians. FA values were greater in the musicians, and a positive correlation with estimates of lifetime total hours practiced was observed.[1]

The other supportive evidence comes from the study of juggling training discussed previously (see under heading Human Studies on Adaptations in Cortical Gray Matter). In this study, participants exhibited enhanced FA values in the white matter of the brain after six weeks of training. However, researchers did not feel that these alterations correlated with performance progress.

On the other hand, neuroscientist Anthony Imfield and colleagues reported that FA values in the corticospinal tracts (the nerve fibers leading from the brain to the spinal cord) of trained musicians were lower than those in nonmusicians.[11] These researchers felt that their findings challenged the concept that augmented accumulation of myelination from sensorimotor practice causes an increase in FA. Jurgen Hanggi and colleagues from the division of neuropsychiatry at the University of Zurich found that professional female ballet dancers had less neural activity in both white and gray matter than did nondancers.[9]

The myelin hypothesis that accounts for improvements in neuromuscular function with training is intriguing and has generated considerable public interest. The idea that banging away on those forehands for an hour a day lays down skill-enhancing myelin is compelling. But just what the thickening of myelin on nerve axons has to do with improving tennis technique is far from clear. Daniel Coyle's contentions in *The Talent Code* that "tennis players . . . get better by gradually improving timing and speed and accuracy . . . by growing more myelin" and that the myelin hypothesis is a "revolutionary scientific discovery" that some consider "the holy grail of acquiring skill" seems a bit premature.[4] To date, no research has demonstrated increased myelin formation in response to physical practice in either animals or humans. Even if this were observed, the dilemma of whether this was caused by, or simply a response to, the training effect would be difficult to sort out.

R. Douglas Fields at the National Institutes of Health has spearheaded research efforts to clarify the role of myelin in training adaptations. He champions the potential importance of adaptations of white matter for motor learning and proposes that "structural changes in white matter could promote learning by improving speed or synchrony of impulse transmission between cortical regions mediating the behavior."[6] He concludes that "learning is not limited to gray matter or to synapses, and structural, electrical, and biochemical mechanisms are all necessarily critical to the cellular mechanisms of learning.[6]

Questions regarding the role of alterations in the brain's white matter and myelin coating of nerves lie at the frontier of understanding training adaptations in sport. Undoubtedly, new research will soon help clarify these issues.

CHAPTER 4

Nature Versus Nurture on the Court

Are champion athletes born or made? Is the elite competitor on the tennis court a product of genetic endowment or the effect of hours of good practice and coaching? Hard-line experts stick with the biological reality of genetic determinism. Popular opinion has embraced the idea that deliberate practice creates star athletes independent of inherent capabilities. The idea that anyone has the power and freedom to become a highly competitive athlete if they just try hard enough is quite attractive. Fence sitters have long been comfortable with a compromise: "It has to be *both*, right?"

This chapter examines these differing points of view and the evidence surrounding each. It first looks at the evidence that one's genes dictate tennis ability and the capacity to improve with training and concludes that everyone has biological limits to physical improvement. It then examines the idea that an individual's athletic destiny is in his own hands and that limits are created only by insufficient intensity, focus, and duration of training. In the end, the reader is free to form an independent opinion—is sports skill a matter of nature or nurture?

In this discussion of nature versus nurture it is tempting to seek insight from the stories of the big names. In the world of tennis are twins with identical genetic material (the Bryan brothers), highly talented siblings (the Williams sisters), individuals from tennis families (Andy Murray), and players who were encouraged by fathers (Andre Agassi) or mothers (Jimmy Connors). Most of these top names started training when they were very young, but others played multiple sports and achieved tennis stardom at a somewhat later age. However, it's treacherous to expect any lessons from such stories. Successful outcomes from early parental involvement, with a family atmosphere that supports and places a high priority on tennis

While the research is still unclear, many nature over nurture advocates point toward the Williams sisters as evidence of genetic endowment playing a more important role in athletic success than intensive training.

Jerry Lai-USA TODAY Sports

success, for instance, could equally be attributed to both genetic and environmental factors. Also, the overall success rates of such efforts at sports training in early childhood are unknown. Player A may have achieved stardom as the result of an intensive training regimen that began at age three, but how many players with a similar story of early stimulation and training failed to find tennis success? Although such stories are intriguing, they don't provide any real insight in the debate of nature versus nurture.

Genetic Endowment

Genes are materials in cells that direct how the body functions. Individuals inherit genes from their parents and pass them along to their children. Kids look " just like dad" or have red hair "just like mom" because the genes that are passed along from generation to generation govern how individuals look and behave. Understanding of the nature of the gene and its functions has evolved in gigantic leaps over the past several decades and undoubtedly is expanding even more. It is worthwhile to briefly review these concepts because in the details it becomes clear how gene function can define athletic ability and an individual's responses to training.

A gene is a segment of deoxyribonucleic acid (DNA) that is located on a structure called a chromosome (a string of *genes)*. This DNA, which comprises two tightly wrapped strands in a double helix configuration, contains nucleotides that code for the production of certain proteins. The protein is not created by DNA itself but rather by ribonucleic acid (RNA) after the RNA has been transcribed from the coded message from DNA. The manufactured protein is then responsible for triggering the function of that particular cell (e.g., making a lens if it's in the eye, making an electrical charge if it's a neuron in the brain, or making bone if it's in the femur).

All individuals have 22 pairs of chromosomes, one string from the mother and one from the father, plus an additional pair of sex chromosomes—two Xs in females and an X and a Y in males. At conception each human begins as one cell, which contains all of this genetic information. During fetal development and into childhood this cell divides and multiplies so many times that an average adult has several trillion cells. All cells in the body (except the sex cells in sperm or an egg) contain the same genetic information.

All cells have the same capacity to fabricate an entire human being. How is it, then, that certain cells make only heart muscle, whereas others produce just ear cartilage or nerve fibers? The quick answer is that cells become specialists during the course of development. Even though they retain the potential for creating proteins to stimulate the formation of the entire human, they restrict themselves to performing a single function.

Because only a small part of a cell's genetic information is being used, it follows that a mechanism for regulating the gene's activity must exist. Figuring out just how this expression of genetic information is regulated has become a major project for genetics researchers. What turns genes off and on?

The information that is in genes dictates the amount of skeletal muscle and number of energy-utilizing mitochondria an individual has. It also affects the formation of synapses and firing rates of neurons in the brain. This is where training comes into play. The goal of training is to alter the expression of those genes to augment these functions. In the end, sport training can be simply reduced to an effort to regulate gene expression.

Multiple highly complex mechanisms are responsible for this gene regulation, and researchers are just now beginning to understand them. Some of the controllers that turn genes off and on are located on the gene itself and others are contained in the associated RNA. As such, they are inherited along with the rest of the genetic material. So, it follows that genes should be expected to serve as principal determinants of both one's basic level of performance ability in sport and one's capacity for improvement with training.

Genetically Determined Potential in Tennis

Many have accepted the traditional contention that an individual's abilities to perform in sport are fixed by his genetic endowment (figure 4.1). Yes, an individual can train, and he will improve, taking advantage of the body's plasticity. However, according to this point of view, this improvement will eventually reach a ceiling created by the chromosomal material inherited from parents.

There are two parts to this argument, both of which are related to the genetic endowment passed on from one's parents. First, it contends that information coded in a person's genetic material largely dictates innate abilities. Intuitively, this stance is not illogical. Genes determine the size of one's circulatory system (endurance performance), the thickness of one's muscles (strength), and one's ability to track a tennis ball and meet it with a swinging racket at a precise moment (the perfect forehand volley). In addition, goes this idea, humans have genes that control the extent to which they can improve with

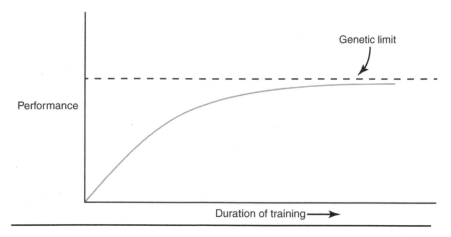

FIGURE 4.1 Traditional athletic curve based on the idea that an athlete's ability is fixed by genetic endowment.

training. Those considered to be high responders adapt to training regimens to a different degree than do those considered to be low responders.

Power Law of Training

In any sport, athletes typically experience impressive increases in improvement in the early stages of a training program. That's motivating. With the proper intervals, duration, and intensity of specific exercise, an athlete gets visibly stronger, runs farther, sprints faster, and plays better. But with continued training, the advances become progressively smaller.

Performance response to tennis practice commonly flattens out over time. This curve, which follows the power law of training, can be expressed as a mathematical equation:

$$Y = aX^{-b}$$

where Y is the performance (e.g., strength, endurance, agility, or another characteristic) and X is the duration of training. It's called a power law because X is raised to the power b, which describes the rate that Y changes with X, and, in this case, makes the curve level off. In this equation "a" is a constant.

As training persists this curve approaches an upper limit (although mathematically it never actually reaches it). Most scientists and sports authorities have traditionally believed that this upper limit of performance is set by the limits of one's genetic endowment.

The power law has undergone many refinements and amendments since it was first introduced in 1926 to describe the curve of performance improvement with training.[5,9] In fact, a wide variety of training–performance curves have been described, with varying means of expressing this relationship over time by mathematical equations. In the research literature, these studies have generally involved non-sport-related skills such as mirror tracing.

This ceiling of improvement after training has been considered to reflect the limits of the biological system, and athletes have traditionally accepted as dogma that physical constraints—be they limits of strength, endurance, speed, or first-serve velocity—limit human performance. There's simply a limit on how fast ions can cross the cell membrane of a neuron to produce an electrical charge or on how fast actin and myosin filaments can slide past each other to effect contraction of a skeletal muscle cell. And the limits of these physiological functions presumably varies between individuals, a variability which can have a genetic basis.

Unless you are an identical twin, you are genetically unique. Because no one else on the planet shares your complement of genetic material, your training–performance curve differs from that of everyone else. As demonstrated in figure 4.1, your rank on the tennis club ladder depends on your upper limit, which, according to the genetic determinism argument, is a function of the genetic tools that dictate both your physical ability and your magnitude of improvement with practice. According to this concept, your responses to training are ultimately limited. Every person is expected to have a different attainable ceiling of performance with training, and this is limit is due to the nature of genetic material inherited from the parents. The rate that improvement occurs with training (that is, the shape of the training-performance curve) can vary for the same reason.

Evidence for Genetic Determinism of Training Effects

Experimental evidence supports the idea that gene function plays a prominent role in athletic training.[4,6,7] Investigations of genetic influence were initially epidemiologic, or population based, particularly by comparisons of physiological function in identical and nonidentical twins. Researchers have moved on to identifying specific gene loci that may be responsible for athletic prowess and training responses. No definitive answers are yet at hand, but it has become abundantly clear that there exists no single fitness gene that dictates athletic prowess. Once again, the complexity of biological functions defies simple explanations. That would certainly hold for a complex activity such as tennis, in which a myriad of visual, neuromuscular, and fitness (both physical and mental) factors are at play.

Epidemiologic Studies

It is important to recognize that no research study has ever undertaken the monumental task of revealing the effects of heredity on one's sport skill. The large number of factors that define skill is simply too overwhelming. Moreover, each factor that would be part of such an analysis—strength, endurance, neuromotor function, visual tracking, visuomotor coincident timing, speed, court sense—is itself potentially influenced by genetic factors. Instead, researchers have focused on uncovering the genetic contribution to individual physiological and anatomical factors that are critical to sport success. Most commonly, such studies have been limited to these specific factors, or phenotypes, listed above that contribute to athletic skill. It's a lot easier to analyze genetic contributions to each of these factors separately with the assumption that, taken collectively, such influences can provide information about the effect of genes on actual athletic performance.

Many modalities of epidemiological testing have been used to estimate the extent to which heredity influences these particular factors. Most commonly, the extent that the determinants of specific individual components of sports skill are shared have been examined in comparisons between groups of sedentary monozygotic (identical) and dizygotic (nonidentical, or fraternal) twins. The former has identical complements of genetic information in their cells, whereas the latter do not. If a particular factor is more closely linked in monozygotic than dizygotic twin pairs, it would indicate a significant genetic influence. Using specific equations, genetics researchers can calculate from the results of such twin comparisons the heritability estimate, or the extent to which genes contribute to the expression of a certain trait.

Let's now examine what these epidemiological studies show about the heritability of the individual phenotypes that contribute to tennis skill.[1,7] Then an attempt at a synthesis can be performed to estimate what, taken together, this information tells us about the genetic influence on the combination of such phenotypes which, in sum, define level of tennis skill.

Maximal Oxygen Uptake

Maximal oxygen uptake ($\dot{V}O_2$max) is defined as the greatest amount of measured oxygen that the body can use when performing an exercise test to exhaustion. $\dot{V}O_2$max is the physiological marker of aerobic fitness and is closely linked to talent in endurance sports in which the athlete relies on oxygen for muscular function, such as distance running, cross-country skiing, and even tennis. As discussed in chapter 8, tennis players typically have greater $\dot{V}O_2$max values than nonathletic persons do because endurance contributes to success on the court, particularly in extended matches.

$\dot{V}O_2$ max itself is an expression of the combined effects of multiple factors, including lung capacity, heart size and function, blood volume, blood hemoglobin concentration, and density of capillaries in the exercising muscle. A few studies have examined the heritability of these individual components of the oxygen-delivery chain, but most have analyzed the collective effect of genes on $\dot{V}O_2$max itself.

The inter-individual similarity of $\dot{V}O_2$max values is about two times greater in studies of monozygotic twins compared with studies of dizygotic twins. This means that the heritability estimate is about 50 percent. This would suggest that genetic determinants account for about one half of the differences between individuals in $\dot{V}O_2$max. Not surprisingly, similar values are obtained when studies have looked at the components of $\dot{V}O_2$max, such as cardiac output, lung function, or heart size, since these factors all contribute to an individual's VO_2max.

When a previously sedentary individual engages in a period of endurance training, $\dot{V}O_2$max usually increases by about 15 to 25 percent. What is striking, though, is the variability of this response. When the eminent geneticist Claude Bouchard and the directors of the HERITAGE Family Study trained nonathletic volunteers for 20 weeks, gains ranged from a liter of oxygen per minute to no gain at all. The researchers posited that the heterogeneity of this response was an expression of individual differences in genetic characteristics.[1]

They subsequently examined this idea by comparing the response in $\dot{V}O_2$max in monozygotic twins using a similar training regimen. The variability of the response between pairs of twins was six to nine times that seen within twin pairs. In another study, the increase in $\dot{V}O_2$max with endurance training between families was 2.1 times greater than that within families. These investigations again revealed a heritability estimate of aerobic response to endurance training of approximately 50 percent. Such findings suggest, then, that the genetic effects on inherent endurance capacity and one's ability to respond with training are substantial and about equal in magnitude.

Somatotype

Officially, only three categories of somatotype exist: ectomorphs (lean and thin), mesomorphs (stocky and muscular), and endomorphs (tend to be overweight). However, some individuals have a mixture of these physical characteristics.

Without question, success in a particular sport is influenced by one's somatotype. That's not to say that all tennis players are built the same way. Excellent players can be short, tall, slender, or squat. But one might expect, for instance, that taller competitors have certain advantages when serving, or those who are lean might have greater on-court fitness.

Imagine the following:

1. The winner of an Olympic marathon
2. The starting left tackle on the Detroit Lions football team
3. A champion gymnast
4. The captain of the Penn State women's volleyball team
5. An elite tennis player

The images that two different people conjure up would likely be similar. These athletes all have different somatotypes, or body builds, and they each have the body structure that fits the needs of their particular sport. The tall volleyball player with long arms was undoubtedly drawn to her sport by her inherent physical characteristics. One can conclude with some confidence that playing volleyball did not make her tall and long limbed.

Is somatotype inherited? Common experience suggests that the answer is yes. Tall, thin fathers can be expected to have tall, thin sons. Genetic studies bear this out. Somatotype is much more closely linked in biological parent–child pairs than in foster parent–adopted child pairs. Interestingly, the level of heritability is usually found to be highest for mesomorphy.

Psychological State

Development of sport expertise with training depends a good deal on the motivation of the athlete coupled with such factors as self-esteem and self-confidence. Sport commentators on television talk about how the team or player who won "wanted it the most." Information on the genetic determinates of psychological state is very limited. Chapter 3 discusses how brain-derived neurotrophic factor, a chemical agent in the brain, might be important in determining motivational behavior and responding to physical training. The gene that triggers the release of this agent has been identified, but research has not yet linked it to sport training in humans.

As will be discussed in the final chapter of this book, psychological state is often critical for tennis success, particularly at higher levels of competition. Whether mental traits such as confidence, high motivation, and ability to focus that lead to greater performance on the court can be achieved through practice, or are, instead, a matter of fixed genetic influence is an important but currently unanswered question.

Other Phenotypes

Here are the heritability findings in studies of other phenotypes which contribute to tennis success. It can be noted that although there is a wide variability among these investigations, the average value is similar for all these traits—about 50 percent.

- **Muscle strength.** Investigations of static strength have revealed widely differing estimates of heritability (0-.83). These studies indicate, interestingly, that strength is more likely passed down from parent to daughter rather than from parent to son. That is, heritability estimates for strength are generally higher in females than in males.
- **Motor performance.** A moderate degree of genetic effect has been observed for activities such as sprinting, vertical jumping, and throwing. Heritability estimates again vary considerably from one study to the next and range from .14 to .91. No sex effect has been observed.
- **Balance.** Few studies have examined the inheritance of balance, but the limited data do not seem to show a large genetic influence. For example, one investigation of beam walking showed correlations between parent and child of only −.01 to +.21.
- **Psychomotor tasks.** Among factors that are important in tennis play, heritability estimates for reaction time range from .22 to .55. In one study of 16-year-old twins, heritability of peripheral nerve conduction velocity was higher (.77).

- **Flexibility.** Limited studies of flexibility have generally demonstrated high heritability (.50-.91) on sit-and-reach tests and other measures of trunk, hip, and shoulder flexibility.
- **Anaerobic (high-burst activity) performance.** Data on anaerobic performance are very limited. In one study of maximal power output during all-out cycling for 10 seconds, correlations between monozygotic twins were .77 to.80, between dizygotic twins were .44 to .58, between biological siblings were .38 to .46, and between adopted siblings were 0 to .06. In this single investigation, genetic influence was high.
- **Motor learning.** Since the beginning of the 20th century, researchers have extensively examined whether genes or environment controls the learning of motor skills. This research has generally focused on the acquisition of fine motor skills or actions that relate to childhood development. Most investigations suggest that the rate of motor learning with practice or training is faster in monozygotic twins than in dizygotic twins. However, once again, the range of heritability estimates is rather wide.

Now let's try to put all these pieces of information together to address the question of a genetic influence on "tennis skill." What do the combined epidemiologic data tell us? It's obviously a bit difficult to say. Certainly they indicate that genetic determinants are important. Overall, the research data suggest that at least half of tennis-playing abilities have a genetic, or inherited basis. But there's obviously a wide variability of heritability estimates, and the data are weakened by the differing research protocols and the frequent failure to consider important confounding variables in these investigations such as age, maturation, habitual activity levels, and body composition. Bottom line: there's a lot of room in inter-individual variability for environmental influences as well. We're all different, and it can be expected that genetic influence on a skill such as tennis, which combines so many various physiologic and anthropometric factors, will vary considerably from one person to the next.

Fitness Genes

Epidemiological data have proven valuable, but things became a lot more interesting in the genetics world when researchers developed techniques for identifying specific gene loci on chromosomes in both animals and humans. This allowed researchers to seek evidence that would support a direct causative link between particular genes and their phenotypic expression. The genetic blueprint, it was forecast, would provide a clear hereditary basis for motor abilities and athletic prowess and would identify specific genes. As research information has accumulated, it has become clear that it won't be quite that simple. However, these data have provided compelling support that genetics has a strong influence on sport performance. At present, none of these identified genes have related specifically to tennis play. However, it is evident that the principles of gene–performance links may have direct applicability to tennis in the future.

The story of the quest to identify genes that relate to physical fitness started about 15 years ago with a study of the gene profile of a group of British mountaineers who were able to climb above an altitude of 7,000 meters without using supplementary oxygen. Researchers found that these highly fit individuals exhibited a higher frequency of a certain form of the angiotensin-converting enzyme (ACE) gene compared with nonathletic participants. This information hit the popular press when such findings were confirmed in rowers and trained Army recruits. Was this the fitness gene?

Maybe not. A subsequent collaborative investigation of highly trained endurance athletes ($\dot{V}O_2$max >75 milliliters per kilogram per minute) from around the world showed no differences in type of ACE gene in these athletes compared with controls. These authors could not support the idea that the form of the ACE gene affected athletic performance. Subsequent reports, however, have again linked expression of the ACE gene to strength training, cardiac hypertrophy, and talent in short-distance events. In another study, investigators found no increase in the ACE gene when Kenyan runners were compared with their nonathletic countrymen. Clearly, the role of the ACE gene in dictating fitness is uncertain.

Such studies have triggered a series of investigations focused on identifying specific genes that might predict athletic abilities, such as the erythropoietin receptor gene, which directs red blood cell production, and skeletal muscle-specific creatine kinase, which is associated with resistance to fatigue during exercise. The list of such candidate genes that influence all aspects of physical fitness has become long. A dozen genes have been identified that are altered in response to a strength-training program. A similar number are associated with increases in $\dot{V}O_2$max with endurance training. At the other end of the spectrum, a review by geneticists Tuomo Rankinen and Claude Bouchard at the Pennington Biomedical Research Center in Baton Rouge lists 23 genes that are associated with exercise intolerance.[8]

Contrary to expectations, the current body of knowledge concerning specific gene action on physical performance has not provided any clear picture of how individual genes might be responsible for a player's prowess in a third set tie break. Many candidate genes exist—hundreds are now on the list— and they have many associations with fitness, but how it all fits together is unclear.

The Nurture Argument

Now let's address the other side of the argument, which says that a person can progressively improve sport skills given the proper intensity, focus, and duration of training. Motivation, access to good coaches and tennis courts, and a family support system are key. According to this argument, no performance ceiling exists to hold an athlete back.

This is the stand held by psychologist Anders Ericsson and his colleagues at Florida State University. Their ideas are twofold: First, effective training, rather than one's genetic gifts, is the dominant influence in establishing sport expertise. Second, this training must be of sufficient duration, quantity, and focused intensity. Simple repetition doesn't work. This concept is not new, but Ericsson, using largely his own research, has outlined for the first time some of the specific details of just what it takes to translate committed, concentrated practice into performance success. He has shown, too, how such deliberate practice might affect the learning curve in a wide range of human domains. He and other devotees are convinced that the willingness to stick to focused training regimens for extended periods of time—not innate genetic talent —makes for elite athletes.[2,3]

Some experts have viewed athletic success as largely situational. When they review the life stories of tennis players who have achieved elite status, they often see early on the perfect combination of fortuitous opportunity, the right coach, and strong support that molds sport success. Still others believe that the roles of motivation and other psychological qualities that permit the self-sacrifice and determination necessary to make it to the top are critical.

Practice-Dictated Skill in Tennis

This chapter has discussed the idea that one's ability to train and improve tennis prowess is governed by the body's biological limits, which are set by the genes handed down from one's parents. Yes, lessons, practice, nutrition, and motivation are each important, goes this argument, but when it comes to improving tennis skills, one can go only so far. The ceiling of athletic performance is fixed.

Ericsson et al say no, that athletes have experienced diminishing returns with continued practice because they have not been training in the right way. With deliberate practice a player can continue to improve to high levels of skill, independent of her genes (figure 4.2). But such deliberate practice takes time and commitment. It takes 10 years and 10,000 hours of training, they say, to perfect a player into an elite athlete. Achieving a high level of athletic success is not dependent on a player's inherent, gene-directed abilities; it's up to the dedication to intensive, focused, long-term practice by the player herself. This is very different than the traditional contention that one is ultimately limited in improvement with

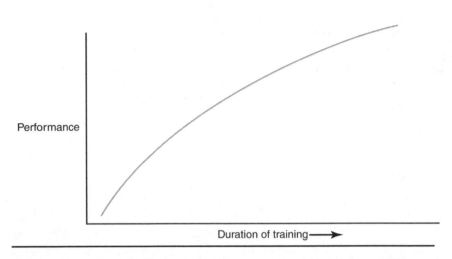

FIGURE 4.2 According to the concept of deliberate practice, improvement gains in performance can be perpetuated, without a genetically-based "ceiling," through proper application of focused, sustained practice.

training via constraints imposed by one's inherited genetic material. Here instead is the idea that the individual player is in control of his sports destiny, that by proper application to training he has the capability of improving sports performance. It's an attractive idea of self-reliance that has captured the attention of athletes everywhere. What follows is a description of the current bases for this argument.

Deliberate Practice

Ericsson and his colleagues argue that according to the nurture argument, the traditional power curve of training (refer to figure 4.1), the typical flattening of the curve of performance outcomes with continued practice is not a reflection of genetically imposed limits. Instead, performance increases stagnate because the athlete is using the wrong kind of practice. The player has taken lessons, watched instructional videos, and practiced with her friends. Her progress has been quite amazing. However, after a while her improvements get smaller. She's making the same mistakes and she's stuck. What does she do? She goes out and plays more, takes lessons, and watches more instructional videos. The fault here, says Ericsson, is that, if one simply engages in the same practice activities repeatedly over time, eventually improvement gains in performance will cease because the workout no longer provides any physiological or cognitive challenges. To progress further it is important to ratchet up the training regimen and create new challenges that demand increased effort and concentration. This is called deliberate practice. With deliberate practice regimens, persistent improvements can boost the athlete to high levels of skill—with no ceiling effect.

Deliberate practice is characterized by

- training that concentrates on specific aspects of performance and focuses on improving particular weaknesses or correcting errors,
- involvement in appropriately challenging tasks,
- hard work (which is typically not enjoyable), and
- ongoing feedback from coaches or experts.

Bottom line: According to this concept, players who want to move up the club tennis ladder have to shift into a focused training regimen with a smart coach. You can't get better, as some try to do, by just playing the game, or by using the same training drills over and over again. Weaknesses need to be identified, and proper practice that challenges those weaknesses needs to be employed. And it takes time for improvement gains. One must be ready to commit to an intensive training regimen for many hours.

Ericsson first became interested in the unexpected effects of intensive training on expertise when he looked at the ability of college students to memorize digits. The traditional dogma held that most people can't remember more than seven digits. However, Ericsson had these participants practice for hundreds of hours and he found that, with this massive training, participants could remember more than 80 digits. Here, he thought, was evidence that limitation of performance with practice is really just the effect of training ineffectively and not training enough. Ericsson believed that the idea that one's genes set an upper boundary for performance achievements with training was wrong and that one can surpass such perceived limits with a sufficient volume of specialized training.

Rules of 10

Part of the doctrine of deliberative practice is the requisite that improvement gains take time. And a magic number of 10,000 hours of training came out of the observational studies of violinists and pianists of Ericsson et al. Their approach was to compare groups with different levels of expertise, assessing practice time and style during their development. For example, in a study of violin students at the Music Academy of West Berlin, Ericsson examined 3 groups of 10 individuals each. The groups consisted of students who were considered skilled enough to have future careers as international soloists (i.e., the best), students who were good violinists but not at the level of the best (i.e., the good), and students in music education who were not high-level performers (i.e., the not so good).

All of the participants had been practicing their instrument for at least 10 years. Self-estimated career-long practice time was directly related to current skill level. At age 20 years, the values were approximately 10,000, 8,000, and 4,000 hours for the best, good, and not-so-good groups, respectively. It was concluded that the volume and type of practice in musicians is related to the level of their performance as adults. Like findings were observed in a similar study of young pianists.

That developing an elite level of expertise usually takes 10 years of training is not simply an outcome of these investigations alone. A decade-long duration has been reported in a wide variety of performance realms, such as analyzing X-rays, evaluating livestock, and playing chess. The studies in musicians imply that deliberate practice over such a duration should entail at least 10,000 practice hours and that one can achieve elite levels of performance with this triad of practice style, frequency, and duration. This flies in the face of conventional wisdom that says one's genetic inheritance won't allow such sustained progress.

Evidence for Practice-Specific Training Effects

When investigators perform similar cross-sectional studies of athletes in both individual (e.g., wrestling, figure skating) and team sports, a similar picture of the time needed to produce elite-level performance emerges: Those who are most talented have practiced more, and it usually takes about 10 years to reach the top of the competitive rankings. The total number of hours before getting there varied from 4,000 to 6,000. Identifying specific issues surrounding time duration of deliberate practice is difficult in such studies because the components of practice differ greatly between individuals and from one sport to the next. One difference, though, is that in contrast to the musicians described by Ericsson, the athletes in such reports tend to report that the hard work of practice is enjoyable rather than onerous.

No research surrounding the role of sustained deliberate practice has been performed in tennis players. Still, the need to continually expand training goals in regard to specific weaknesses and strengths in the hands of a competent coach certainly resonates with those seeking to improve their tennis skills.

Nature and Nurture

Some factors that define sport success are clearly genetic in nature, such as body height, sex, and somatotype. An obese teenager is not likely to succeed in training for the school gymnastics team, and a skinny beanpole will see little success in training to be an interior lineman on the football team.

The demands of persistent deliberate practice that is carried on for 10 years are challenging. Not all can put up with the rigors, sacrifice, and commitment required to achieve this. That's why so few elite-level athletes exist. Ericsson concedes that the right mental equipment is necessary to sustain such an extended, intensive training regimen and that the psychological qualities surrounding a sustained, long-term commitment to the hard work of deliberate practice that makes for a champion just might be under genetic control. This pivotal issue is revisited in chapter 10.

Those engaging in the labors of deliberate practice to sustain performance improvements walk a fine line between too much and too little. Some researchers have suggested that deliberate practice beyond one to two hours a day may provide no benefits. The athlete who pushes her body beyond its physiological limits without sufficient rest to allow adaptation is at risk for physical injury and deterioration of performance (i.e., burnout). The efforts to perform deliberate practice must be wisely constrained to prevent these outcomes, which are clearly antithetical to performance goals.

Deliberate practice involves other practical matters as well. One must obtain the services of an expert coach to provide guidance and feedback over a long-term period. Family and peers must offer a strong network of social support. Parents need to provide transportation to practice sessions. And, in many cases, the weather must cooperate.

Some detractors feel that insufficient evidence has been provided to support the deliberate practice model proposed by Ericsson et al. Their concerns include the following:

1. The scientific basis for the deliberate practice model is weak. Ericsson and others have taken a group of highly successful performers and retrospectively looked at the characteristics of their training. This is a very limited perspective. What about the athletes who adopted this regimen—a decade of deliberate practice—and failed to achieve a high level of success? This critical piece of information is nowhere in the argument.

2. Over the years, thousands of very talented young tennis players have been enrolled in expensive training academies. This is a highly selective group participating in tightly controlled conditions under the supervision of expert specialist coaches. Training is highly focused and is performed for many hours a day for many years; this clearly satisfies the requirements for deliberate practice. Emotional and social-support mechanisms are built into

the training. It is hard to imagine programs that more directly satisfy Ericsson's concept of the form of training required to reach elite levels. These academies are justifiably proud of the superstars they've created. However, among the thousands of participants, those who have made it to the top are a very small minority. One by one, participants have fallen by the wayside and failed to join the elite at the top of the rankings.

3. The direction of the arrow of causality—what causes what?—in Ericsson's studies of musicians and the investigations of athletes is not clear. For instance, if it is observed that an association exists between lifetime accumulated practice hours and level of skill, this relationship is assumed to indicate that the former is responsible for the latter. But would it not be just as reasonable to expect that the opposite might be true? An individual who has greater talent and who is awaiting high-level competitions and performances might be motivated to practice more. People are motivated by what they do well. And might the talented performer be more likely to attach himself to a better teacher, have access to better facilities, and use better equipment? Success breeds success.

4. Ericsson's studies fail to take into account the possible wide variation in individual responses to training. In studies of skill at darts and chess, training factors accounted for only about one third of individual variability in performance.

Summary

Is it nature or nurture, or maybe both, that makes the champion athlete? Both sides of this debate have marshaled a good deal of compelling evidence to support the idea that genetic potential—or, alternatively, extended duration of effective training—is the key element in the development of athletic success. However, I suggest that neither side has provided a convincing argument that their model serves as the limiting factor of one's ultimate potential to reach a high level of athletic success.

From the genetics perspective, we see that genetic expression is key to defining both skill and the ability to improve with training. (Ericsson et al. would agree that these are the expected mechanisms for improvements associated with deliberate practice.) But to assume that an individual's genes limit her ability to improve with fitness requires an assumption of physiological and anatomical limiting factors. Maybe you've reached the limits of speed of nerve conduction, or protein synthesis in the muscle, or velocity of sliding of actin–myosin filaments. But, biologists have not yet provided information that defines the upper limits of such function. Thus, it is not possible to state with confidence that a ceiling of genetically controlled physiological function defines the upper boundary of one's ability to improve performance with training.

There are other observations, too, that are not consistent with the genetic model. For example, one sees outliers, people who succeed in sports without a history of athleticism in the family. The heretability studies have provided rather divergent results. It is now seems clear that no specific individual fitness genes exist—performance in sports is just too complex.

The advocates of deliberate practice need more science too. The idea that one needs to practice hard to achieve success and that such practice has to be extended, focused, challenging, and appropriate to one's stage of development, along with the idea that one needs good coaching, social support, and the right motivational frame of mind, makes good sense. But will it work for everyone or only for those with certain genetically based inclinations, either physical or mental? The nurture camp has not answered this important question. Retrospective studies of two or three groups of a small number of performers divided by present skill to determine such issues as hours of practice (based on recollections of 15 years in the past) are not a satisfactory means for addressing the issue. Prospective randomized studies in which groups are divided by style and duration of training are needed to assess performance outcomes.

The ideas of Ericsson and his colleagues are attractive, if nothing more, from the standpoint of their emphasis on individual responsibility—free will—in determining athletic success rather than a genetic pre-determinism. Consequently, the concept of deliberate practice and 10,000 hour rule have rapidly become adopted in the popular domain. But there are many questions yet to be addressed. In tennis, for example, how do such principles dictate areas of practice focus? For instance, if you practice a forehand for 10,000 hours, you would probably develop a pretty devastating forehand, but you still might not know how to play the game. If all this sustained practice is necessary and fruitful, how can it be made more enjoyable? What are the down-sides—risk for injury and mental and physical fatigue, leading to dropout from sport? And in the next chapter we'll address the question of how the deliberate practice concept is—or is not—consistent with proper goals of sports training in childhood. Clearly much more needs to be learned.

CHAPTER 5

Player Development

In May of 1992, when returning from a conference, I had the pleasure of sharing a taxi with Tudor Bompa. Professor Bompa came to the United States after years of developing his innovative and highly successful coaching methods in his native Romania. There he trained 11 Olympic medalists and was largely responsible for the competitive success of the Eastern Bloc countries over three decades. He has been called the world's leading specialist in training concepts, particularly in respect to periodization, and his ideas have had considerable impact on the most appropriate means of sports training during the childhood years. According to Bompa:

> We really can't be treating children like they were small adults. If kids focus in on a particular sport early on, yes, they'll show fast improvement. But that's a narrow approach to children's sports. For the long run, they need to take time to form a good base by developing fundamental motor skills. Without this, it's like trying to build a high-rise building on a poor foundation.

> It takes time to develop a good athlete. Proper training begins in childhood but not with a rush to specialize in a particular sport. Coaches need to recognize that kids are in a process of developing, physically and psychologically, and we need to provide training regimens to fit these changes.

At the meeting, Bompa had discoursed on one of his favorite topics: the wisdom (or, rather, lack thereof) of the trend for early specialization in youth sports. In his half hour he provided a passionate, convincing argument that narrowing in on a single sport at a very young age—even if a child is extraordinarily talented—quite simply is not appropriate. Instead, he's an outspoken advocate of multilateral development, in which the would-be child athlete is introduced early on to athletic programs that emphasize the general development of motor skills. Bompa contends that focusing on a single sport should come later—even into the teen years.

When I returned home, I noted in the local newspaper a feature story on young boys who were preparing for a big upcoming boxing tournament. The next day, during a visit to a park, I witnessed five-year-old baseball hopefuls, fully uniformed, following the instructions of their coach while the usual dutiful crowd of proud parents watched. On television I viewed a documentary on Canadian traveling youth hockey teams made up of players who were too young to read or write. The question of early versus late sport specialization and the ubiquitous focus on competition in young child athletes has been forever bounced back and forth by sport scientists, developmental psychologists, coaches, exercise physiologists, and sociologists. The debate has spawned books, doctoral dissertations, scientific workshops, and articles in the Sunday newspaper. From these has arisen a barrage of arguments—along with sophisticated psychological models, laboratory physiological research, and abundant expert opinion—surrounding the scientific aspects of developmental training programs.

And then there's the real world. People in the real world—parents with precocious children, aggressive coaches building reputations, professional scouts on the prowl, national Olympic committees seeking gold—are not listening to all this. They have not encountered Tudor Bompa. They have other agendas. It seems that coaches, parents, and children are convinced that the only way to create superior young athletes is to have them play only one sport from an early age and to play it all year round.

For better or worse, the insatiable drive for sport success has begat early sport specialization in child athletes. Competition in adult-organized sport programs and the lure of athletic stardom have progressively lowered bar on the age at which specialized training in athletics begins. Sport psychologist Dan Gould at Michigan State University has termed this the professionalization of youth sports.

This chapter avoids the question of the possible inappropriateness of all this emphasis on early sports training and specialization in youth from the standpoints of issues such as ethics, child abuse, and even violation of child labor laws. A great number of people are certainly concerned about these matters. These pages instead examine what the experts have to say. However, it's important to remember that such a discussion must be set in the context of the powerful cultural forces that have influenced trends in youth sports.

This chapter also examines some topics that are part of this early quest for producing highly skilled athletes. The people who want to develop children into athletes at an early age place considerable emphasis on adult-directed competitive teams, which were unheard of 50 years ago. One crucial issue in such development of young athletes is early talent recognition, or picking out at an early age the player who is destined for sport success. Finally, the chapter looks at what makes for successful tennis development by comparing programs in countries that have been highly effective in producing top athletes against those with less success.

Developmental Tracks

Your daughter Sarah has shown some rather astounding tennis ability, even when first picking up a play racket. By age 8 she was out on the courts, displaying aptitude on both the forehand and backhand sides and competing with players almost twice her age. At age 10, it is clear that she is blessed with extraordinary talent. She wins the club under-12 tournament, and you know she could beat high school players as well. Sarah loves to play, and you have to drag her away from the courts. How do you, a responsible parent, respond to Sarah's talent?

Is it your duty to allow and encourage your daughter to fulfill her given talents? Do you say yes and think about signing her up with the club pro, enrolling her in a tennis camp, making the tour of the tournaments, or budgeting for a tennis academy? Or do you say that she can play tennis now, sure, but that you'll enroll her in other activities and sports as well and then think about focusing on tennis when she gets into her early teens? Sarah is undoubtedly destined to be a great tennis performer, but she has about 10 years to go before she might work her way to the top. That's a long time, particularly for a youngster who is supposed to be developing in many other ways—socially, psychologically, and physically— and you worry that she may burn out and lose her enthusiasm for the game. Or worse, she could begin suffering nagging overuse injuries that sideline so many great players. Yes, she will miss some tournaments and trophies now, but that's a small price to pay for long-term success.

So there's a difficult choice to make here. Let's examine how the experts have viewed the advantages and disadvantages of each of these pathways toward developing excellence in sports.

Option 1: Early Sport Specialization

The literature suggests that it takes at least 10 years to produce a champion athlete in most sports. If so, that means that the athlete must start out on this road early on.[3,13] This is particularly true for sports in which peak performance is expected during the second decade of life, such as gymnastics. If top international gymnastics competition gives out top scores to competitors in their late teens, it doesn't take much arithmetic to figure out that training must start by age seven. Those who follow the theory of deliberate practice (outlined in chapter 4) believe that this approach is the only way to reach the elite strata of the competitive gymnastics world. They claim that, in accord with the theory of deliberate practice, early specialization is necessary in order to train at the duration and intensity required to produce elite-level talent at an appropriate age.

According to Anders Ericsson and his co-workers:

There is ample evidence that children and adolescents do not spontaneously engage in the deliberate practice that ultimately leads to maximal performance. Consequently, children need help to identify the appropriate training activities, to learn how to concentrate, and to find the optimal training environments.[10]

He goes on to state, "Elite performers generally start training in their domain of expertise early, and are given access to superior training resources at very young ages." And, goes the argument, if child athletes do not get into a program of early specialized training, they will be left behind by those who do. Still, he concedes, there are limitations:

When one considers the prerequisite motivation nec-essary to engage in deliberate practice every day for years and decades, when most children and adolescents of similar ages engage in play and leisure, the real con-straints on the acquisition of expert performance become apparent.[10]

Ericsson and others have pointed out that critical periods for motor development and acquisition of sport skills may exist during childhood and that such periods would signal a need for early sport specialization and focused practice. Such periods are vague concepts rather than scientifically documented pro-cesses. However, some have suggested, for instance, that the development of myelin coating of peripheral nerves with training might be more prominent during childhood. (This could lead to greater training effects, as noted in chapter 3.)

At young ages it is the parent who initiates this process and ultimately becomes responsible for the emotional, financial, and transportation needs of the child during early training ex-periences. In many life stories of elite performers, a single parent or other significant individual has taken on such a de-cisive role and is considered the driving force for the ride to the top. Some such individuals view this as matter of personal responsibility. In his autobiography, John McEnroe quotes Richard Williams, coach and father of Serena and Venus Williams:

> Look, I picked something great for them, something that'll give them a tremendous living and a tremendous life. It's crazy to think that they were capable of making that decision when they were young. So, of course I pushed them, but they needed to be pushed.[14]

Case in point: Andre Agassi has hit tennis balls for as long as he can remember. In his crib his father hung balls from a mobile and encouraged his infant son to strike at them with ping pong paddles attached to his hands. By age 7 he daily volleyed a required 2,500 balls delivered by a ball machine that he called "the dragon." Sometimes, instead of driving him to school, his father would divert to the courts for a half day of play. Tournament play started at age 8, when he won 7 of his first 10 competitions in the under-10 category. By age 10 he was on the national circuit.[2]

Option 2: Multilateral Early Training

Delaying specialized training in a single sport is the dictum of those who believe in a holistic approach to the development of sport talent, which considers the developmental immaturity of the growing child. This is Tudor Bompa's stance: Young children need to develop fundamental motor skills—speed, endurance, coordination, flexibility, and strength—before being exposed to training in specific sport skills for which they are not adequately prepared. This gestational period also allows for the marked variability in rate of physical development in children. Late maturers are not penalized in the sport-selection process and early maturers, normally spotted by the coach first, do not gain inappropriate attention.

 Bompa envisages this process as a pyramid (figure 5.1) in which multilateral development in the early childhood years gives way to specialized training in adolescence, followed by more high-performance training later on.[4] The tempo of this

FIGURE 5.1 The pyramid of development of athletic skill during the growing years, based on a base of multilateral involvement rather than early sport specialization.

Adapted, by permission, from T.O. Bompa and M.C. Carrera, 2005, *Periodization training for sports*, 2nd ed. (Champaign, IL: Human Kinetics), 58.

process is dictated by the sport involved, but the foundation is always laid down first for basic overall fitness and the development of basic motor skills. This allows for a normal progression of developmental adaptation in the child and guards against early burnout and overuse injury. According to this viewpoint, such early diversification permits the general development of physical movement, fitness, and perceptual skills that can be applied to any sport in later years.

A good number of experts have supported Bompa on this position. Jean Coté, an associate professor in the school of physical and health education at Queen's University in Kingston, Canada, and colleagues introduced the term *deliberate play* to express what they viewed as the optimal approach to early sport training in children.[6] They characterized deliberate play as the intermediary between the free play of very young children and the deliberate practice of the adolescent and older athlete as proscribed by Ericsson. Deliberate play, they contend, involves the following:

- Play behavior that is performed for its own sake and is not constrained by rules or social demands
- Physical activities that are fun and bring pleasure to the child
- Activity that is motivated by the performance of the exercise and not by results or outcomes (i.e., winning or losing)

The idea is that sport training for children should evolve during the growing years and that its focus should be altered as the athlete ages. This is completely compatible with the recognized course of cognitive, physical, emotional, and social development during the childhood years. In their survey studies of successful athletes, Cote´ and others emphasize how other factors surrounding the development of the childhood athlete, such as coaches and parental involvement, follow the same evolutionary pattern of childhood development. For example, tennis coaches of six- to eight-year-olds do not need to be experts in their sport. Instead, they need to know how to deal with the immaturities of young kids and how to instill in them the joy of physical movement. However, in the teen years, expert coaching becomes essential. The role of parents throughout the different stages usually changes as well, from encouragement and instruction in early years to support and organization in later years.

This approach is not dissimilar to the multilateral model, proposed by Tudor Bompa, which calls for progressive changes in the content and goals of training, the types of expertise of the coach, and the role of the family. It also fits nicely into a philosophy of taking it easy during the early stages of introducing children to sport in order to instill an enjoyment of sport and to stay compatible with the physical and psychological developmental changes that occur as children mature.

As its promoters emphasize, this period of progressive involvement in sports is not simply a time for developing physical skills. It's also a time for creating a mental approach to playing games that provide the future athlete the psychological skills to permit the long-term commitments demanded by deliberate training. According to this approach, the role of stimulating in motivation cannot be underestimated and formulating a positive mental state in young athletes is as important to early training as developing sport-specific skills.

Case in point: Björn Borg is the son of an expert table tennis player. Borg was a very good athlete as a youth but reportedly never picked up a tennis racket until he was 9 years old. He decided at age 13 to abandon his first sport passions—

Shown here in a moment of triumph after winning his fifth-straight title in the men's singles final at Wimbledon, Björn Borg decided to focus solely on tennis at an older age than many other professionals.

Colorsport/Icon SMI

ice hockey and soccer—to concentrate on tennis after he won some tournaments in his native Sweden, reasoning that he had never won a big tournament playing hockey.

Picking a Path

No good science exists that could help resolve the conflict between options 1 and 2. Little is known for sure about how sport skills are best acquired during childhood development. It seems that the way to settle the issue is to examine the life stories of celebrated tennis players and define the pathway that led to their success, and a number of authors have done just that.

However, this doesn't resolve the conflict. What is missing is an assessment of the developing athletes, whether early or late specializers, who failed to achieve high success. What is needed to answer the question is a large study that divides randomly selected five-year-old would-be athletes into early- and late-specialization groups and assesses the outcomes. That study will probably never be done due to the complexity of a long-term longitudinal study with multiple complicating variables.

Retrospective analyses have revealed some interesting points about the early training stories of star athletes. In 1985, Judith Monsaas published a detailed analysis of the course of development of 18 players from the United States who ranked among the world's top 10 between 1968 and 1979. It must be acknowledged that the nature of the game—and particularly its financial rewards and societal status—were very different than they are today.[15] However, the findings are likely still pertinent.

To start, the great majority (75 percent) of those analyzed came from close-knit, tennis-playing families who spent a good deal of time at tennis or country clubs. These families valued commitment to hard work and dedication to always doing one's best. Introduction to tennis was quite automatic (the average age of starting to play was six years) and part of normal family activities. Despite this, initial tennis play was entirely recreational; none of the players studied reported having any designs on a professional tennis career. The majority played other sports until the age of 12 years. Most began competing in tournaments at about this age and, after achieving success in these competitions, began focusing on tennis seriously in the early teen years. At this point, coaches became an increasingly important part of the players' development. The stories of these elite players was for the most part quite stereotypical: strong family involvement early on, delayed specialization, key coaching, and the psychological characteristics of determination to work hard, extreme competitiveness, and a hatred of losing.

In 1999, Coté found a three-stage development pattern when he interviewed elite junior tennis players. In the first stage, parents introduced children to sport between the ages of 6 and 12 years (called the "sampling years"), with a focus on achieving fundamental motor skills, enjoyment, and excitement.[6] Player commitment toward tennis increasingly involved during the second stage. In the third stage, the player entered the teen years and training and competition began seriously.

The arguments for a multilateral approach are persuasive but they are based on retrospective information obtained several decades ago. Do they hold true for the development of skilled athletes in the high-pressure world of elite athletes today? Or does the accelerated drive to achieve the top levels in sport almost demand an approach of early specialization? Has early specialization become a fact of life for child athletes who are following the dictates of parents, coaches, and sports governing bodies as well as cultural expectations? I tracked down Tudor Bompa in Toronto, where he is now professor emeritus at York University, and asked him those questions. He replied:

> There is no doubt we are seeing a grave cultural pressure on coaches and young athletes to achieve at an earlier age, and that's made for increasing earlier sports specialization as well. This need to "succeed," with emphasis on winning, places a great deal of stress on children—exag-

gerated by the coach's own desire to prove his or her expertise. We see in that the win–loss statistics kept on different coaches.

For all the reasons put forth in the past, the multilateral training program is still the most developmentally appropriate approach. But one particular benefit that I see as I witness outcomes of early specialization–early competitive sports teams for children today is that a multilateral program results in a reduction of injury rate. All that early training that we see is producing an increasing number of overuse injuries in young athletes. (Personal communication)

Returning to young Sarah, your precocious star tennis player, just how do you, her parent, interpret the contradictory approaches to helping her develop her talent? Should it be through early specialization? Or a delayed multilateral approach? This author, admitting a bias as a pediatrician, sees the delayed, multilateral approach to be a more healthy and—in the end—more productive one. But he's never had a star tennis-playing daughter, either. Parents need to weigh the pros and cons and select what they see, according to their own philosophy, of which pathway is best.

Early Talent Identification

Can one take a 9-year-old boy, run him through a battery of physical tests, and, based on the results, predict what kind of athlete he will be in 10 years? Coaches and sport administrators hope the answer is yes. They want to invest their time, effort, and money in those who are going to make the grade. A great deal of research attention has been focused on creating such a crystal ball. After decades of experience, trying this and trying that, what is the success rate?

By the traditional model, one's athletic skills are to a large extent defined by genetic factors and one's genetic makeup is stable. Therefore, by deductive reasoning, skills manifested at age 9 should be good indicators of skills that will be present at age 19. Or so has been everyone's expectation.

It comes as a bit of a surprise, then, that experts such as kinesiologist Werner Helsen and colleagues at the Katholieke Universiteit in Leuven, Belgium, come to the conclusion that "at present, it is difficult to support the notion that sport expertise can be predicted on the basis of any specific measure of talent."[11]

That remarkable statement comes from a study by Helsen and colleagues that examined the roles of biological development and practice in expertise in soccer players. But, then, maybe it isn't all that surprising. Consider the following:

- The statistical odds are stacked against accurate early identification of future sport talent. That's true even as late as the adolescent years. As sport scientist Bob Malina points out, more than half a million boys play high school basketball in the United States, yet among these only several dozen eventually are drafted onto professional teams.[11] Statistically speaking, a weary scout visiting high school games around the country would have chance of spotting 1 future star among every 12,000 players he watched. At the middle school level, the odds would be maybe twice as bad.
- Level of sport talent in youths is often a matter of the extent of their biological maturation. As children grow they normally become larger, stronger, and faster. In fact, virtually all the components that go into skill in a particular sport evolve over the growing years. And—here's the rub—a dramatic difference exists in the curves of performance improvement from one child to the next. At any given chronological age, then, the level of talent in a sport will vary considerably due to individual differences in level of biological maturation. At one end of the spectrum will be the early maturers, who are most skilled, and at the other end will be those who are developing late.

The coach of a fifth-grade football team will understandably put the early maturers on the first team and the later maturers on the bench. However, there is no way to tell which of these players will ultimately be the best players down the road. It's not astonishing, then, that Helsen and colleagues concluded that "we suspect that early maturation or physical precocity is one important characteristic that forms the basis of early talent selection".[11] One can see that by this misleading influence on coaches success in early talent identification becomes so tenuous.

This issue comes up when one finds among high-level adult athletes a trend for birth date to occur in the first part of any given year. The supposition—though not proven—is that these people were among the early maturers in their school days and received more attention, encouragement, and playing time from coaches in the initial stages of their athletic training. By itself that's no great surprise, but what is intriguing is that this advantage persists into the adult years, when the advantageous effect of early maturation on sport skill is gone. Perhaps all that early attention from coaches has a lasting effect, or, alternatively, perhaps the slow maturers simply became discouraged and headed off for careers elsewhere.

As outlined above, the traditional schema that forms the basis for early talent identification presumes a strong genetic effect on sport skills. That is, it requires the existence of innate talent. But as chapter 4 shows, the sentiment is growing that extrinsic factors (e.g., amount of effective practice, accessibility to a good coach, the support of family) coupled with a particular psychological capacity for motivation and commitment are what really make champion athletes. Advocates of this line of thinking say that genetic limits are not really part of the picture.

The role of psychological factors—motivation, persistence, self-confidence, adaptation to hard work—is usually ignored in early talent screening programs. But we're getting a bit ahead of the story here. Let's go back and examine just how early talent identification has been attempted in the past and then assess the success of such efforts. The key issue here is whether the results of efforts to recognize early-on future sports stars support the discouraging conclusions of Helsen and his soccer players. We can then go out on a limb and ask some daring questions: Is there *any* way to predict future athletic performance in youngsters? Or should we just give up?

Approaches to Talent Identification

Historically, two principal approaches have been used when attempting to identify at an early age the child athlete who is destined for sport stardom. The first approach relies on screening young children for physical qualities that are expected to be major determinants of success in a particular sport. In tennis, for example, agility, speed, balance, eye–hand coordination, muscle endurance, and rapid reflexes are important to expert performance on the court. The six-year-old who scores high in a test of these elements gets picked for tracking into early tennis training.

Such testing has been devised for a number of sports. Its predictive value clearly depends on a number of questionable assumptions: The components of the test must truly relate to performance in that sport, and the child's scores on a given component must be stable over time. Moreover, the chance that certain weaknesses can be compensated by strengths in other components is ignored.

In the past, this method was characteristic of programs in Eastern European countries in a wide variety of sports. More recently, it has been employed by China and Australia. Certain gold medal successes can be cited, of course, but as sport scientist Bob Malina points out in an interview in *The Athlete's Clock*:

> You only hear about the successes, and you don't know the denominator in the equation to calculate success. The basis of this approach, of course, lies in the assumption that early sports-related traits are predictive of those later on. The problem is, there is no way such a supposition can be expected . . . . Overall the predictive value of early testing batteries has to be very low. [16]

The second approach to early talent identification is what can be called the "cream will rise to the top" method. With mass participation in a sport (such as swimming) at an early age, the most talented identify themselves as they grow older. Coaches and sport administrators keep a close eye on this progression and are quick to direct those with performance success into specialized training in that sport. This is the method commonly used in countries with large populations, such as the United States.

Bompa has emphasized a particular problem with this approach: The identification of a child destined for success in a particular sport depends on whether he chose to participate in that sport at an early age. That leads to the assumption that many youths have the potential for elite performance in a sport that they just didn't happen to try.

Without knowing failure rates, there is no way to scientifically determine whether either of these approaches are actually successful. Some veteran coaches claim that their years of experience have given them a sense of who is going to make it big and who will not. However, most experts remain highly skeptical and believe that, based on the current perspective, the ability to predict a young athlete's potential for future improvement and ultimate success based on current performance is low.

Alternative Predictive Qualities

Recognizing the weaknesses of profiling young athletes in order to predict sport success, numerous authors have recommended focusing instead on the ability of the child to develop in response to training. These authors believe that the young athlete's capacity to learn a sport provides the most accurate insight into future performance and that one must distinguish between performance and skill at a young age and the capacity to develop over time. They recommend abandoning early talent identification and replacing it with opportunities to develop the skills that go into sport excellence, and they state that the monitoring of that process provides the best chance of identifying those who will go on to future stardom. However, the logistics of such an approach for sport organizations, which are under heavy financial and resource constraints, seem to be highly problematic.

Writing in *Journal of Sports Sciences*, Angela Abbott and Dave Collins of the department of physical education, sport and leisure studies at the University of Edinburgh argued that "a range of psychological behaviors appears to underpin a person's true potential for [athletic] growth" and that such variables have had "insufficient consideration" in approaches to talent identification.[1] Abundant evidence, largely in nonathletic domains, supports the idea that psychological traits strongly influence performance success. Chapter 4 specifically proposes that in the deliberate practice model a young athlete's motivation to stay committed to long-term intensive training programs may be a key factor in the development of performance. Abbott and Collins conclude that any model that attempts early talent identification needs to include psychological attributes.

Although not specifically studied in young tennis players, the applicability of these concepts to developing competitors on the court is apparent. Success in the competitive arena lies heavily on one's ability to stay tough in tight tennis matches as well as a mind-set that withstands the grueling hours of practice.

Tennis-Development Programs

This chapter would not be complete without examining what happens in programs specifically designed to hoist young tennis players from the exceptional to the elite ranks of international competition. These are called player-development programs, and every major country on the international competitive scene has its own. The goal is to take hundreds of highly skilled junior players and advance them to the professional level. The success of these programs can be measured by the top player rankings, which supposedly offer objective proof that some particular training scheme separates the tennis skills of one country over those of another.

Some programs have more money or more luxurious accommodations than others, but they all have highly motivating and skilled coaches, involve a ton of practice, and combine all the ingredients that supposedly go into producing talent (e.g., technique, fitness, mental concentration). It's difficult to identify just what differentiates the program of one country from that of another. Daniel Coyle, who wrote *The Talent Code*, had the same reaction when he traveled to the renowned Spartak Tennis Club in Moscow in 2006 to determine just what accounted for the Russians' astounding success in international tennis competition.[8] At that time 5 of the top 10 female players in the world were Russian, as were 12 of the top 50. Why? Many opinions had been put forth: a superior Slavic gene pool, new role models (starting with Anna Kournikova), a president who loved tennis, and the softness or lack of discipline of Western players.

Coyle found the tennis club in a desolate section out in the suburbs. It had a single indoor court and unpredictable heating, and wooden sticks supported the net to a proper height. There he watched the legendary 77-year-old Russian coach Larisa Preobrazhenskaya put 5- to 7-year-old hopefuls through their drills. He wrote in *The New York Times*:

> Seeing the place up close made me wonder if there were any principles. Even here at the core of one of the globe's brightest blooms, the question of that talent's source remains enigmatically tangled, perhaps as much of a mystery to those who nurture these athletes as it is to the rest of us. It's enough to make you wish for a set of X-ray glasses that could reveal how these invisible forces of culture, history, genes, practice, coaching, and belief work together to form that elemental material we call talent—to wish that science could come up with a way to see talent as a substance as tangible as muscle and bone, and whose inner working we could someday attempt to understand.[8]

The United States Tennis Association has carefully created a comprehensive player-development program that involves regional centers, highly skilled coaches, and countless outdoor courts. According to its mission statement as stated on the USTA website (www.usta.com), the program is devised "to develop world-class American players through a clearly defined training structure and competitive pathway as well though the implementation of a comprehensive coaching philosophy and structure." It's a well-oiled machine that by all considerations should be churning out players holding trophies over their heads at the Slams. However, the output has been disappointing to many critics. Currently, only 3 male players from the United States rank among the top 50 in the world. On a per capita basis, the Iberian Peninsula is producing 10 times as many elite male tennis players as is the United States.

For decades in Great Britain, attention at any given moment has been limited to a single highly competitive player. What has been the problem with British tennis? Why can't the British Lawn Tennis Association and the All England Croquet and Lawn Tennis Club (which, in addition to trying to identify and develop young talent, runs Wimbledon) deliver championship players more often than once every 75 years? Many believe that the problem is at the grass roots and that tennis clubs are not producing any young players with sufficient skill and desire to go further in the sport. These critics say that these clubs are still working on an antiquated idea that they should exist as social, rather than performance-driven, organizations. Player development is not high on their agenda; a friendly over-40 mixed doubles tournament is. Then there's the problem of money. Considering the perpetual glum of drizzle, chill, and wind on the island, indoor courts are a very costly necessity. Others believe that the tournament schedule, which would motivate junior players into staying with the game, is inadequate.

What about Spain? Behind Rafael Nadal the list of successful Spaniards, particularly the men, is impressive. In 2012 I traveled to Barcelona, where most eventually come to train, to ask Sacra Morejon—player, coach, and trainer of coaches—about the secret of the Spanish success. Morejon replied:

I don't think it's really just one thing. But to start with, we create a strong base of young tennis players because of the easy accessibility to courts throughout the country. And then we have some very successful models that encourage our youth. They say, if he can do it, why not me?

We tend to focus a lot on developing technique, and that's somewhat unique in Spain because unlike many other countries we have a great many clay courts. Successful play on clay requires particular attention to technique, particularly combined with patience and strategy.

Spain has an extensive number of well-organized tournaments for young players. When I asked Morejon whether she thinks that early success in tennis tournament play is a good way to predict future success, she laughed and replied with this story: "When Rafa Nadal was about 15 years old, he won a very competitive tournament here in Barcelona. His coach, Uncle Toni, was concerned that Rafa might be getting a big head over the victory. 'Rafa, here is a list of 15 names. Tell me how many you recognize.' Rafa looked over the list with a puzzled look. He couldn't identify any of them. 'These,' said Uncle Toni, 'are the last 15 players who won this tournament.'"

Bill Dwyre, sport columnist at *The Los Angeles Times*, presented a critical perspective on this angst surrounding the failure of various national player-development programs to produce elite-level products. He says that we fans appreciate elite tennis players as individuals with remarkable athletic skill and we find joy in watching them go up against others who are equally endowed. Are matters of patriotism really as critical as some believe? Dwyre contends:

Measuring and establishing credit for player development is impossible, even silly. All the weeping and gnashing of teeth over who does what for whom, and who should get the pat on the back, is much more political and guilt-soothing than is real. The real point is that, although U.S. tennis fans like a nice homegrown face on their center court at key moments, they are fine with anybody from anywhere who is a great player, has a great personality, and provides great entertainment. Will the 25,000 people filing into Arthur Ashe Stadium on a Sunday for a Rafael Nadal–Roger Federer final do so with long faces and feelings of being shortchanged, one being from Spain and the other from Switzerland? Of course not. [8]

Why elite players at the top of the international rankings come from one country or another often has no clear explanation. It cannot be explained simply by the extent of a country's developmental programs. At the time of this writing, the top elite players come from countries such as Switzerland, Serbia, Denmark, and Belarus—nations not known for their player-development programs—as well as countries where such programs are strong, such as Spain, France, and Russia. In 10 years the rankings of countries with top players will probably be all different. Some would say that nationalism in the world of professional tennis competition is misplaced and that tennis is an individual sport in which fans find joy in watching, admiring, and emulating extraordinary athletic skill that goes beyond national boundaries.

Certainly from any analysis that can be made comparing such development programs, there does not seem to be any one or more "magic" means of developing tennis stars. Perhaps this can be some consolation to the average club player who is struggling to find just that "missing ingredient" that will get him to the top of the club ladder. The best conclusion: Everybody is different—we all learn differently, have different capabilities, and, ultimately, different limits.

CHAPTER 6

Physics of Tennis

The game of tennis, far from being a simple racket sport of polite aggression, is best viewed as a vicious contest between two highly complex neuromuscular systems on opposite sides of the court. Most of the time these machines are on automatic and working beneath the level of consciousness. They battle it out under not only the strict rules of the game but also the firm laws of physical motion.

This chapter addresses these immutable physical principles that govern the game—as well as the motions of heavenly bodies and everything else that surrounds our lives. Whatever tennis players do—train, stay hydrated, improve physical fitness, or develop mental toughness—these laws remain set in stone. Still, players have an opportunity to improve performance out on the court by understanding these physical rules and appreciating how they can be used to one's advantage.

This chapter begins by describing the laws of motion as set for tennis players by Sir Isaac Newton. It then discusses Daniel Venturi, whose tennis skills are unknown but who provided important insight into the physical laws that influence the game, particularly the spin of the ball. Finally, the chapter looks at a few examples of how recognizing these physical constraints can give players an advantage. Controlling physics might just pay dividends.

Newton's Laws

Isaac Newton was born in 1642 at Woolsthorpe Manor in the United Kingdom, about 60 miles (96.6 km) northwest of Cambridge, where he later attended Trinity College. An isolated and introverted but extremely inventive student, he developed his early ideas of gravitation, calculus, and optics during the two years the school was closed due to an outbreak of the bubonic plague.[4] Chemist William Cropper describes Newton as the greatest creative genius in physics.

Most people associate Newton with the discovery of gravity. Of course, the presence of gravity was no secret before his time. What Newton uniquely provided was the insight that the force that causes objects such as a tennis ball or an apple to fall to the ground is the same one that influences the motions of the planets and causes the tides to change with the orbit of the moon. He defined universal gravitation and developed a mathematical expression that accurately predicts this attraction between bodies, both on the tennis court and in distant galaxies. Interestingly, though, Newton provided no insight into the nature of gravity or what causes it. Exactly what gravity is remains a mystery to this day.

When playing tennis one endeavors to adjust the direction and force of each shot to account for this force of gravity. Through experience, the automatic player has memorized Newton's equations and has learned to translate them into just the right angle of racket attack and force when striking the ball. The flight of the ball obeys Newton's laws of motion. His law states:

> To every action there is always opposed an equal reaction: or, the mutual actions of two bodies upon each other are always equal and directed to contrary parts.

The clearest example of this idea is the strong recoil of a fired rifle. This action and reaction happens on the tennis court, too. When the ball strikes the court and then bounces away, the ground it strikes recoils in the opposite direction. That is, when it hits the court, a high-bouncing lob actually causes the entire planet to budge just a bit. Of course, the mass of the Earth is so much greater than that of the ball that the amount of this displacement is infinitesimally small.

The same expression of this law occurs when a player strikes the ball with a racket. As the ball's direction is reversed when it leaves the racket, an identical force pushes the racket and the player backward. The player doesn't feel this because of the friction (or braking effect) of his shoes on the court. As the science writer K.C. Cole points out, if the player were playing tennis on roller skates, he would roll backward each time he hit the ball, and it wouldn't be long before he ended up in the parking lot.[3]

According to Newton, given a stationary racket (like when one is blocking back a tough serve), the angle at which the ball arrives at the racket face will be the same as that when it leaves. This certainly adds to the challenge of returning an effective, well-placed shot, so racket manufacturers have endeavored to design racket faces that reduce the angle of the ball's exit. They "violate" Newton's law by reducing the amount that the racket twists on impact. This decreases the angle of rebound and gives the player more control of the shot.

Here's another of Newton's laws:

Every body continues in its state of rest or of uniform motion in a right (straight) line unless it is compelled to change that state by forces impressed upon it.

Suppose you hit a high looping forehand toward your opponent. If no additional forces acted on the ball, the ball's inertia would cause it to continue to ascend—out of the court, through the layers of the Earth's atmosphere, past the orbits of Neptune and Uranus, and toward the outer galaxies. The ultimate mis-hit. But, of course, your ball is acted on by gravity, which causes it to arc downward and, hopefully, land into the other court just out of reach of your opponent.

Indeed, the force and angle that you applied to the ball will be carefully calculated by your neuromuscular machinery—using Newton's equations—to do just that. You have transferred this Newtonian law of motion—balancing the magnitude of the effect of the force applied to the ball by the racquet to the downward force of gravity—into a winning shot.

So now that we can appreciate all this science that dictates tennis play we can move on to looking at some examples where a player can actually make use of this information to gain advantages on the court.

Science of Spin

Everywhere, things spin—heavenly bodies, subatomic particles, children's toys, gyroscopes. Spinning is a fundamental action of the natural world. Our planet revolves as well, at a speed of about 1,000 miles (1,609.3 km) per hour at the equator. It's a good thing that the atmosphere, glued to the surface by the force of gravity, rotates with it at the same speed. If it didn't, a ball tossed to serve at Flushing Meadows would be somewhere just outside Trenton by the time a player reached to hit it. Fortunately, the ball moves at the same speed as the rest of the planet and stays in the same position relative to the player. Tennis players can use an understanding of the physics of spin to modify to their advantage the effects of gravity on their strokes.[9]

When applied to a tennis ball, spin creates uneven forces that alter the course of the ball through the air. A spinning ball can skid at midcourt or cause a lob headed for the players' box to suddenly drop like a stone on the service line. It is almost impossible to strike a ball without applying any spin whatsoever, but manipulating strokes by purposefully applying spin can make one a master of the game.

Our understanding of spin comes from Daniel Bernoulli, an 18th century mathematician working at the University of Basel. Bernoulli's principle states that the faster a gas or fluid is flowing, the lower its pressure. This principle is best explained in terms of how airplanes fly. The wing of a 747 is cambered so that the curvature is greater on the top than on the bottom. Because the same amount of air flows over both the top and bottom of the wing as the plane flies, the air on top must flow faster. (It has farther to go due to the curvature, yet in the same time duration as the air beneath the wing.) According to the principle, the slower-moving air on the bottom has greater pressure than the air on the top, and the wing is pushed up.

Topspin

The same thing happens when a tennis ball is made to spin as it sails across the court. Imagine you're looking at the ball from the side and it's moving from left to right. If the ball is not spinning, the air pressure above and below the ball will be equal and the only action in the vertical direction will be gravity, which causes the ball to fall as it passes over the net. But if a player hits a forehand so that the ball is spinning counterclockwise from your viewpoint, the air just at the surface of the ball will be spinning as well. The air at the top of the ball directly meets the surrounding air as the ball travels, sort of like a headwind. Conversely, the air attached to the bottom of the ball moves in the same direction as the air it meets, like a tailwind. As a result, the air at the bottom of the ball travels faster than that at the top. According to Bernoulli, the pressure on the top of the ball will be greater than that underneath as it flies over the net. This will make the ball dive, or curve downward, rather than follow a straight path (figure 6.1).

That's topspin. Applying this type of rotation to the ball causes it to land short of where it would by gravity alone.

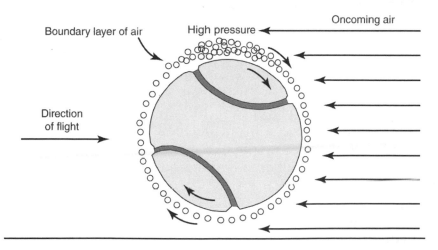

FIGURE 6.1 The Bernoulli effect when a ball is hit with topspin.

Reprinted from J. Groppel, 1992, *High tech tennis*, 2nd ed. (Champaign, IL: Human Kinetics), 111, by permission of the author.

Then, when the ball does strike the court, another altered action takes place: It bounces higher. As discussed previously, the angle at which a ball rebounds is normally about the same as the angle at which it hits the court. If it arrives at 60 degrees relative to the near court, it departs at 60 degrees relative to the far court. However, a ball hit with topspin comes down more vertically than a ball that's not spinning does. Consequently, it rises more abruptly. When the ball is struck briskly, it bounces up with greater speed.

Topspin is created when a player sweeps the racket face up and over the top of the ball. A ball hit is this fashion dips up (because the racket face moves up to strike the ball), falls shorter, and rebounds higher and with greater velocity. The ball can be struck safely by the player with greater velocity.

Among the most common mistakes that a tennis player commits are vertical errors, or errors of depth. The ball must be struck within the angular window of acceptance, defined as the range of angle of the ball leaving the racquet that will allow it to both cross safely over the net yet still land in the opponent's court. This window is affected by several factors, including the height of the contact point, where on the court the ball is struck, and—most important—how hard the ball is hit. Physicist Harold Brody discovered that the window of acceptance shrinks by about half when a ball is struck at a speed of 70 mph compared to that leaving the racquet at 50 mph.[1,2] This means that slowing the velocity of the ball improves the chances for a good shot. However, no player wants to help his opponent by slowing the ball. This is where topspin helps. Using topspin, the player can hit the ball harder but the window of acceptance will not decrease as much as it would with a flat stroke because the ball will be less likely to go long. Topspin makes the ball drop earlier and keeps hard-hit strokes in the court.

Björn Borg was the first real master of topspin, and with his enormous success the shot quickly caught on. Borg had his rackets strung extremely tightly—a tension of about 80 pounds per square inch. His powerful shots would rise to pass about 6 feet (1.8 m) above the net but then rapidly plummet to drop well within the baseline. His opponents said it was impossible to get any rhythm going against him while defending shots like that. Today's game, with its emphasis on power shots delivered from the baseline that Borg pioneered, would be quite impossible without reliable topspin to keep the ball in the court.

Backspin

Imagine that, instead of sweeping up and over the ball to create topspin, a player strikes the ball in the opposite manner, carving the racket down and under. Now the ball spins in the opposite direction, causing it to strike the other side of the court at a very shallow angle and then skid forward and low (figure 6.2). Such a slice shot is more difficult for the opponent to deal with because she has to swing up on it. This increases the margin for error; that is, the window of acceptance is diminished. That's particularly true for an opponent using a two-hand backhand because she has to scoop and lift the shot. This then gives the player a better chance for a put-away volley at the net. A slice that is delivered deep to the opponent followed

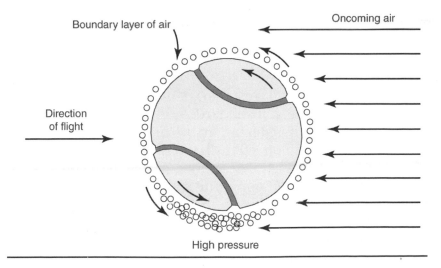

FIGURE 6.2   The Bernoulli effect when a ball is hit with backspin.

Reprinted from J. Groppel, 1992, *High tech tennis*, 2nd ed. (Champaign, IL: Human Kinetics), 111, by permission of the author.

by a rush to the net—the old "chip and charge" that brought John McEnroe so much success—is a good strategy.

In today's power game a well-delivered slice is still an effective shot, since as the ball bounces low and typically skids on the court, it is more difficult for the returning player to apply topspin to her shot. Also, tall players, favored particularly in their serve velocity, may have a more difficult time stooping down to reach a sliced shot.

Warning: This will work only if the sliced shot is struck aggressively and flies low over the net. The softer a slice is struck, the more likely it will rise higher and drop short in the opponent's court. This misfortune will cause it to rise vertically and lazily, sitting up for the opponent. If this occurs, the player who hit the ball probably should immediately duck and cover.

Reducing Errors of Laterality

We've talked above about how one might avoid errors of depth, or hitting the ball long. And we've seen that these could be avoided by (a) reducing the velocity of the shot, and (b) applying topspin. But what about keeping the ball from going wide, so-called "errors of laterality"? Again, there are several strategies that, according to Dr. Brody and his colleagues, might be employed.[2,3]

The first, a matter simply of common sense, is to attempt to direct the ball toward the center of the opponent's court. When you do this, you have a margin of error of almost $10°$ on each side and the ball will still land safely in. Boring, but safe. The second means of reducing errors of laterality is to direct your shot in the same direction that it arrived. Your opponent strikes the ball from her left corner of the backcourt, then that's where you should aim your return shot. What you are trying to do is avoid changing the angle of the ball when it leaves your racquet from that upon which it arrived. You swing the racquet head perpendicular to the flight of the oncoming ball, and you want to have it fire off your racquet strings at that same perpendicular angle.

Newton told us that the angle of incidence (the angle the ball arrives) is the same as the angle of reflection (the angle is bounces off the strings). But here's an important lesson. Sir Isaac was not right, or at least not all the time. If the ball arrives perpendicular to face (that is, 90°), it will leave at 90°. But if you try to alter the angle of the shot, the angle it leaves will vary, and that will depend on how hard you strike the ball. The harder you hit a ball arriving at 90°, the closer the ball will leave from the perpendicular. But if you hit it softer, the ball angle leaving increases, and the softer you strike it, the greater the angle, and thus the greater the chance of the ball spraying out in some misdirection. That's why players who are out to a comfortable lead, when trying to "play it safe" by decreasing the force of their shots, can find a ball aimed down the line end up wide in the alley. And winning momentum is lost. Hitting softly increases errors of laterality by augmenting the angle the ball flies off the racquet. And all this despite what Newton said. The morale: keep hitting out!

Fine. You can keep ball from landing wide by (a) aiming for the middle portion of the opponent's side of the court, (b) returning the ball in the same direction from which it arrived, and (c) maintaining good racquet head speed. But, you know, that's OK if you're playing strictly a defensive game of tennis. Most of us, though, play for the thrill of the winning shot, the elation of catching your opponent off balance, of strategizing to place balls at amazing and unreachable angles. The excitement is in the offense. The above principles will allow you to make less errors, both vertically and laterally, but if this is all you did, they would make your game dull and predictable. The challenge of the game is knowing when to gamble. The odds of making a successful inside-out forehand that leaves the racquet at an incredible angle (and your opponent flat-footed) might be, say, 1:4. Do you take the risk? Making that decision is a fun part of the game.

Playing With Physics

How high should one toss the ball when serving? Where should one stand when returning the serve? Where is it best to return a shot hit to the baseline corner? The answers to these queries, of course, depend on many factors, but behind them all lie some basic principles that govern the motion of moving bodies. Recognizing these laws of motion can help out on the court.

First-Serve Percentage

Striking an accurately placed, sharply hit first serve is not an easy task. Even the world's best players are content to be successful about two thirds of the time. Yet those who excel at hitting a well-placed, booming first serve have an effective weapon at all levels of tennis play. Perfecting a serve comes down to hours of committed practice, but some underlying principles may provide helpful keys to success. It all comes down to angles and spins.

During the serve, one wants to increase the angle of acceptance so that the ball clears the net but allows the tug of gravity to cause it to drop in front of the opponent's service line. Hitting with high velocity will narrow the angle because there is less time for gravity to catch hold of the ball and bring it into the service box. Most players try to accomplish high speed on the first serve because it catches the opponent off guard, giving him less time to react and increasing the chance of an error on the return.

Striking the first serve hard increases the chance of winning the point if the ball goes in, yet reduces the chance of the ball going in. A player can increase her first-serve percentage by holding back on the speed, but that comes at a price. Indeed, success in serving is a matter of a number of tradeoff decisions regarding serve velocity, the height of the toss, and application of topspin.

Play Tall

Even to the casual tennis fan, it's apparent that tall players tend to have incredibly powerful serves. The higher one strikes the ball on the serve toss, the larger the angle of acceptance will be and the greater the chance the ball will clear the net and still not land long outside the service box. Brody and colleagues performed a computer calculation of this effect, which indicated that the acceptance window of a serve of 120 miles

Using his tall, muscular frame, Croatian star Ivo Karlovic can crank out scorching serves, as he's about to do here at the 2011 SAP Open.

Phil Carter-USA TODAY Sports

(193.1 km) per hour struck at a height of 9.5 feet (2.9 m) is four times greater than that of a serve struck at a height of 7.5 feet (2.3 m) (1.3 degrees versus .3 degree).

It's not just a coincidence, then, that the tallest male player on the professional circuit as of this writing, the Croatian Ivo Karlovic, holds the record for the fastest serve delivered: 156 miles (251.1 km) per hour. Karlovic stands 6 feet 10 inches tall (208.3 cm), wears size 16 shoes, and was briefly in the record books for the greatest number of service aces (77) in a Davis Cup match against Radek Stepanek. (This occurred before the epic 11-hour marathon match between John Isner, 6 feet 9 inches (205.7 cm), and Nicolas Mahut, 6 feet 3 inches (190.5 cm), at Wimbledon in 2010. During that match these guys fired 113 and 103 service aces, respectively.)

As part of a more in-depth analysis of this phenomenon, Rehett Allain an associate professor of physics at Southeastern Louisiana University, posted on the Internet a compilation of the fastest serves on record and the players' heights (table 6.1). As expected, the height at which these tall players strike the serve provides a greater margin of error, thus permitting them the luxury of increasing ball speed beyond that which would decrease the chances of a successful serve in a shorter player. Allain underscored this point by constructing a graph that plotted fastest serve versus player height in which he included players of smaller stature. This graph revealed a moderately close relationship between the serve speed and player height. According to the graph, though, the relationship is not linear. If it were, a player who was 1 inch (2.5 cm) tall would be able to serve the ball at 68 kilometers per hour.

Do the longer arms of the tall player increase the ability to generate racket and serve speed? I posed this question to Dr. Joseph Hamill, biomechanist at the University of Massachusetts. He replied:

> Being tall, with long arms, gives the server a huge advantage in terms of generating ball speed. The linear velocity imparted to the racket at the end of the arm is the end product of the angular velocity and the length of the

TABLE 6.1 Comparison of Height and Serve Speed in Male Tennis Players

Player	Height (m)	Fastest serve (km/h)
Ivo Karlovic	2.08	251
Andy Roddick	1.88	249
Milos Raonic	1.96	246
Joachim Johansson	1.98	245
Taylor Dent	1.88	241
Greg Rusedski	1.93	240
Marat Safin	1.94	235
Fernando Verdasco	1.88	232
John Isner	2.06	232

Data from R. Allain, 2011, "Does the fastest tennis serve depend on height?" [Online]. Available: http://www.wired.com/wiredscience/2011/03/does-the-fastest-tennis-serve-depend-on-height/ [November 19, 2013].

upper extremity segments. The angular velocity may be the same in a short and tall player, but the length of the arm is obviously greater in the latter. Within the upper extremity, too, the velocities at the segment endpoints are additive. The movements of the wrist, forearm, and upper arm during the serve will all be greater if you're taller.[6]

The peak velocity of the racket during a serve varies from 60 to 80 miles (96.6-128.7 km) per hour. So, if you want to fire first serves at the high range with a bigger angle for success, be tall. If you don't happen to be so genetically gifted, at least *play* tall. Stand erect and toss the ball high. However, standing tall is not the only element in becoming a superb player with a devastating serve. Witness names such as Federer, Borg, and Sampras, all who stand about 6 feet 1 inch (185.4 cm).

Strike High

Lacking genetic tallness, the next best thing for the server is to vertically extend his body as high as possible to hit the ball. The higher the toss and the higher the player stretches to hit it, the greater the window of acceptance. Brody and colleagues contend that hitting the ball flat-footed reduces the chance of a successful first serve by 30 percent:

> Every extra inch (2.5 cm) of impact height corresponds to about a 5 percent increase in the first-serve percentage for the average player hitting a 100 miles (160.9 km) per hour serve, so even an increase of a single inch will be significant in the course of an entire match.[2]

A few other things might help improve serve speed. A player can use a longer racket, strike the ball high on the racket face, or grasp the racket lower on the handle.

Should a player jump into the air when reaching to strike the serve? That would seem to add at least a few inches in the quest for an altitude advantage and increase the chances for serve success. It is probably true that all skilled tennis players jump into the air when executing the first serve. However, professional tennis coach and sport biomechanist Jack Groppel thinks that this jump is a result of the momentum developed in delivering the serve rather a conscious act on the part of the player. He contends that actively jumping into the serve may be disadvantageous:

> To attempt a purposeful and forceful upward jump when serving would require a unique amount of coordination and inhibit the tennis player's attempt to hit an effective serve. Therefore, we should not consider the leaping action seen during the serves of many world class competitors as a necessity for hitting a good serve.[5]

Hit Topspin

In the same way that topspin increases the window of acceptance for a groundstroke, the looping, downward trajectory of a serve hit with topspin offers an opportunity for increasing first-serve percentage with balls hit at high velocity. The trick, however, is tossing the ball up in the air and providing the appropriate spin while extending the body upward. Quite simply, performing a topspin serve is not easy. One must sweep upward yet forward over the ball while it is descending, a biomechanical feat that requires much practice and a good deal of neuromuscular skill.

Strike on the Descent

A traditional way of hitting a serve has been to toss the ball high and then stretch to strike it as it reaches its zenith. Optimally, the player will hit the ball when it is actually stationary, which makes striking and directing the ball with confidence easier. However, another technique permits one to strike the serve with some topspin without really trying. If the player strikes the tossed ball with a perfectly flat stroke (i.e., without trying to apply any spin whatsoever) while it is descending in its path, some topspin will automatically be applied. The faster the ball is falling, the greater this effect. To accomplish this the player has to toss the ball high, above the height she can stretch to reach it and then strike it as it is falling—but still as high as she can. The result is applied topspin, a greater window of acceptance, and a faster serve.

Professor Brody and colleagues have studied this too. They found that if a player tossed the ball just 6 inches (15.2 cm) above the point of impact, the number of serves going in increased by 12 percent. If a player tossed it 15 inches (38.1 cm) higher than you can reach it, the number of serves going in increased by 25 percent.[2]

This strategy does have limits. Most particularly, the higher a player tosses the ball, the faster it will be falling when the player hits it and the more difficult it will be to coordinate the shot.

Returning Serve

A lot goes into the decision of where to position one's self to return the serve. Some positioning is predictable: about at the baseline to return an average serve, a few steps back to return a cannonball-type serve, and forward, maybe even to just behind the service line, for a weak serve or a slow second serve. If a player figures wrong, she can adjust quickly for the next service point. However, if the player receives a high-kicking serve it might be best for her to move forward to keep the ball from ascending to shoulder height (or more) before she can strike it. Moving forward is also as a good strategy if the player is planning an aggressive rush to the net with the return.

Among the factors that influence where to stand on a return, a central theme is that a player wants to have sufficient time to respond effectively to the oncoming serve. Just how much time does a player have? Brody calculated the time it takes to react to a flat, down-the-middle serve traveling 110 miles (177 km) per hour.[2] A player crouched at the baseline has .65 second to react, whereas a player awaiting the serve 5 feet (1.5 m) inside the baseline has .59 second. If the player has retreated to 5 feet behind the baseline, the time increases to .71 second. A distance of 5 feet in where a player stands for the serve return alters the response time available by about 10 percent.

In order to create a successful serve return in that span of .6 to .7 second, the player has to track the flight of the ball, decide how to hit it, coordinate muscular action to create the return stroke, provide exquisite timing such that the speed of the swinging racket exactly matches that of the oncoming ball, and strike the ball with appropriate racket angle and force (and with spin) so that it flies back in a 20 degree arc. How do tennis players achieve this? Three factors, all of which have been measured in the laboratory research setting, can be examined: simple reaction time, coincident timing, and use of anticipatory cues.

Reaction Time

Simple reaction time is the time it takes for a participant in the laboratory setting to press a button in response to a light or auditory stimulus. It's called simple because only one motor response has to be made and no decision making is involved. The simple reaction time represents the time it takes for (a) visual or sensory nerves to transmit a signal to the brain, (b) central processing of this information within the brain, (c) nerve transmission to the finger muscles and (d) muscles to contract and push the button. The average simple reaction time is about .2 second. Because this time reflects the limits of electrochemical events that limit nerve transmission, it is not surprising that this value is pretty fixed. It is similar in athletes and nonathletes and probably is not influenced much by repeated trials (i.e., training).

The story is different when it comes to applied reaction time, or the time it takes to respond to a stimulus that is specific to a particular sport (e.g., swing a bat to hit a pitched baseball, adjust to return a tennis serve, or block a penalty shot). These reaction times in a given sport are shorter in athletes who are highly skilled in that particular sport than in nonathletes or athletes who play other sports. Although it could never be ruled out that innate rapid reaction times of stellar competitors enable them to be better athletes, common experience and some research indicates that training improves such applied reaction times.

Research has divulged some interesting information regarding reaction times. For instance, reaction times become longer with age, particularly after age 50, and during the middle years of life reaction times are about 25 percent slower in females than in males.

In a study by Tim Mead and colleagues of the health and physical education department at Nicholls State University in Louisiana, a voice from a computer told a tennis player that he had made a "nice shot" or a "bad shot."[7] The player's reaction time to a subsequent computer-generated video ball was faster after he received the positive feedback than when he received the negative feedback.

Professor Jui-Hung Tu and colleagues from the National Pingtung University of Education in Taiwan studied the effect of two factors in 18 college players —how well the court is lit and the speed of the oncoming ball—on reaction times to volley at the net. They measured reaction times to a ball projected by a machine at high (25 meters/second) and slow (18 meters/second) speeds in high- and low-illumination conditions. Intriguingly, they found that reaction times to make a volley were faster in the low-illumination condition and when the oncoming shot was faster. These authors hypothesized that these findings reflected the players' greater level of attention when the lighting was dim and that "better coordination between central processes and muscle contractions in a well-trained athlete will be aroused when the incoming ball velocity is increased."[10]

Anticipatory Cues

Experienced tennis players gain advantage by anticipating the direction, speed, and type of shot, which reduces reliance on neuromuscular reaction time. Much of this comes from knowing the play patterns of particular players. Knowing that in a certain game situation player A is likely to serve out wide can increase player B's chances for a successful return. Or maybe A knows that player C is particularly notorious for an up-the-T serve when the score is his advantage.

Researchers have also shown that the top players learn how to anticipate certain shots by focusing on certain visual aspects of the opponent, such as body position, orientation of the racket, and motion of body segments. For example, skilled players seem to focus more on the server's arm and racket than novice players do. Professor Jaeho Shim and colleagues at Baylor University demonstrated that hiding information about the motion of the racket and forearm significantly reduced skilled players' accuracy in anticipating shots.[8] Just how expert players learn to predict shots is uncertain. Some feel it's a consequence of recognizing opponents' movement patterns through repeated play and practice, whereas others have suggested that such abilities reflect the acquisition of a set of holistic visual-processing skills.

Returning a Ball Hit With Spin

As discussed earlier in the chapter, a ball hit with topspin can be hit harder and still descend within the court, whereas a slice becomes a low, skidding ball. This section looks at the other side of the story—how a ball that arrives with spin affects a player's return.

The observant player can derive a good deal of anticipatory information from watching how his opponent strikes the ball. The kind of spin put on the ball determines the path of the ball in the air, the angle and speed at which it will bounce, and the spin it will have after it rebounds in the player's court. Table 6.2 summarizes the actions of a ball hit with spin on a medium-paced (i.e., not slow clay or fast grass) court.[2]

When a ball strikes the court, some topspin is automatically applied due to the slowing effect of friction on the underside of the ball. That's why even a flat serve rebounds with some topspin. It is easier to return a ball hit either flat or with topspin by the opponent by striking it with underspin, which makes the ball spin in the same direction it was spinning when it arrived. Hitting a flat or topspin shot with topspin takes more force because the player will be required to reverse the direction that the ball is spinning. Trying to hit a sliced shot with underspin is difficult because the player has to lift the ball higher to get it to clear the net and has to impart more energy

TABLE 6.2   Effects of Spin on the Ball Path

Spin	Path after bounce	Final spin
Underspin (slice)	Low and skidding	No rotation
Flat	Straight	Topspin (30 revolutions)
Topspin	High and fast	Topspin (70 revolutions)

Adapted from H. Brody, R. Cross, and C. Lindsey, 2002, *The physics and technology of tennis* (Vista, CA: Racquet Tech Publishing).

to the ball to get it to spin. The bottom line: By paying close attention to how the opponent strikes the ball, players have less chance of being taken by surprise as it bounces off the court toward them.

Hitting From the Corner

Players have always been taught that, in general, a ball hit to one's corner at the baseline should be redirected over the center of the net rather than down the line. That's because directing the ball down the line requires lofting the ball over the highest part of the net, which is 3 feet 6 inches (106.7 cm) high at the sideline but only 3 feet (91.4 cm) high at the center. That seems to make sense. However, according to Brody, the ball has to travel farther to get over the center (41 feet [12.5 m] versus 36 feet [11 m] down the line). This gives gravity more time to cause the ball to descend. In fact, if the net were the same height all the way across, a player would have to hit the ball higher to get it to clear the net down the middle than to send it down the line.

The player has to consider two factors. One, it's farther from the corner to the center, which requires hitting the ball higher, and, two, the net is higher down the line, which again requires hitting the ball higher. It's probable that in most situations the two factors cancel each other out, meaning that from the standpoint of net clearance there's no advantage in returning the ball to the center instead of down the line, although players have a much bigger target of court space if they return the ball down the center. A little personal experimentation with these two directional tactics might help resolve the issue.

CHAPTER 7

Tennis Technology

The inventiveness of humans has always affected the games they play. From shoe design to retractable roofs, technological innovations have advanced and defined the modern game of tennis. This chapter addresses three of these developments: the evolution of the lightweight, easy-to-string racket; the challenges created by court surfaces, from the high-speed hard court to slow-bouncing clay; and the advent of automated, computer-based line calls that provide the game with a new level of accuracy at the professional level. The topics are often controversial, backed by very limited scientific data, and open to the subjective interpretation of individual players.

Modern Tennis Racket

Every once in a while I take my old Wilson Jack Kramer wooden racket out of the closet, unscrew the wooden press that keeps it from warping when it rains, and take a few practice swings. I haven't struck a tennis ball with this racket for more than 35 years and I won't now, fearing that the now-brittle strings would snap. The Wilson Sporting Goods people sold more than 10 million of these beauties between the 1948 and 1981. It is the most popular racket ever made. People like Arthur Ashe, John McEnroe, and Tracy Austin won big using it.

Over time, steel, aluminum, fiberglass, and composite graphite replaced wood and frames got lighter, stiffer, and bigger. Advances in racket technology have undoubtedly dictated the evolution of tennis toward the powerful baseline game of today. Recreational players are benefactors of this new technology, and with rackets that are easier to swing and more gentle to muscles and tendons, older players can stay with the game even at advanced ages.

Purchasing a tennis racket used to be simple. Pick the grip size, choose gut or nylon strings, indicate the desired stringing tension, and you were good to go. But no more. The following sections touch on all the factors one might consider when preparing for a racket purchase.

Weight

Weight is important. A player can get a lightweight racket that weighs about 240 grams or can go with something heavier—all the way up to more than 320 grams. For comparison, the wooden Jack Kramer racket weighed 400 grams. A wooden racket provides more power and is less shocking to the arms. Because a heavier racket rotates, or twists, less than a lighter racket, it gives players better control over shots when the ball strikes the racket face off center. The downside is that the major factor in determining how fast the ball comes off the racket is not the weight but rather the speed of the racket. The faster a player swings, the faster the ball flies off the racket. One can swing a lighter racket faster than a heavier one. The end result—the power of the shot—is about the same. Therefore, the speed of the racket swing is not the same thing as the power the swing generates. Those who like to come to the net often will do better with a racket on the lighter side because they allow a player to react quickly when volleying. The heavy racket works best for those who sit at the baseline and bang away.

Things get a bit more complicated when considering what happens when a player swings a racket. The swing weight is the amount of torque (work) that one has to use to swing the racket. A racket with a high swing weight will be harder to swing and won't be as maneuverable as one with a lower swing weight. The weight of the racket is not the only factor that determines swing weight. Other factors are involved, such as the location of the balance point (the center of gravity or center of mass) of the racket. If the balance point is located toward the head of the racket, the racket is head heavy. If that point is located toward the handle, the racket is head light.

Head-heavy rackets have a greater swing weight; they're harder to swing but generate more power and stability. Head-light rackets have a lower swing weight; they're easier to maneuver and swing faster. A player can swing a head-light racket faster or a head-heavy racket slower and get the same speed of the ball coming off the racket. Players who can generate powerful strokes should note that at a given swing speed, a heavy racket that is head heavy generates more power. Putting some lead tape at the head of the racket makes it more head heavy.

Dimensions

A mid-size racket has a face of 80 to 90 square inches (516.1-580.6 cm^2), and an oversize racket has a face of up to 115 square inches (741.9 cm^2). Then there's an oversized racket that measures 120 square inches (774.2 cm^2)—surely a far cry from that old wooden racket that measures 60 to 80 square inches (387.1-516.1 cm^2). Other than getting lighter, the big change in rackets that occurred about 30 years ago was the growth of racket size. Players quickly bought into this change because the bigger head caused a significant increase in the size of the sweet spot and moved the sweet spot closer to the exact center of the racket face. Players said that the larger racket was more forgiving; specifically, it decreased the occurrence of erratic shots hit off center. The bigger head also provided more power. The designers said that a large racket would also twist less, which meant less stress to the arm.

Some find these really big rackets to be cumbersome and less maneuverable. Others think that the wider rackets actually lead to greater twist on the wrist because the ball can be struck farther off the center of the face; this can lead to tennis elbow and other overuse injuries. These are reasons why the pros don't use these rackets. Some tennis experts have even suggested that playing better with a big racket is just psychological and that the improvement in performance is all in the player's head.

The standard length of a racket is about 27 inches (68.6 cm). A longer racket provides more power and more spin, and it helps players reach for shots better. However, along with extra length come less control, not as much maneuverability, and greater shock to the arm. Rules set by the International Tennis Federation limit racket length to 29 inches (73.6 cm) or less.

Composition and Stiffness

Wood, aluminum, and fiberglass have come and gone. Almost all rackets today are made of carbon (graphite) fibers combined with a polymer resin or something else. The end result is a racket that's a lot lighter and good deal stiffer than the old Jack Kramer. In some rackets the carbon fibers are covered by a layer of titanium. The advantage of titanium is that it is equally strong in all directions, whereas graphite is tough only in the direction of the fiber. The disadvantage of titanium is that it's not as light or stiff as graphite.

Manufacturers usually classify rackets as stiff, medium flexible, and flexible. Stiffer rackets can produce higher ball velocities because they don't bend as much at ball contact. Most people think, though, that a flexible racket provides better ball control. Stiffer rackets have a bigger sweet spot, but they also transmit more shock to the arm.

Sweet Spot

Players typically think of the sweet spot of the racket as the place in the middle of the strings where the ball flies off easily, with no vibration or shock, and goes right where one wants it to. According to scientists, a racket actually has three sweet spots, and they're not all in the same place on the face.[3,10]

The first sweet spot is the center of percussion—the region where the shock the hands feel upon striking the ball is least. Although this spot is usually located near the center of the racket face, its location depends to some extent on where on the handle the player grips the racket. The second spot is the node—the place where vibration is minimized. It's not a point, actually, but rather a line that runs horizontally through the center of the racket face beginning at the 10 o'clock position on the frame and ending at the 2 o'clock position. The best place to hit the ball is the point at which this line intersects the long axis of the racket; hitting the ball there results in little vibration and less racket rotation. The third spot is the place where the ball is returned with the highest velocity. Scientists talk about the coefficient of restitution, which is the ratio of the speed of the ball arriving to the speed of the ball leaving. The higher this value, the more power the racquet can impart to the ball. This spot is usually low on the racket face, toward the throat. Because most players try to hit the ball in the center of the racket, manufacturers have devised ways (i.e., adding weight to the head, making the head stiffer, or designing a wider head at the top) to move this sweet spot further up on the racket so that it coincides with the node.

On a typical modern racket, the three sweet spots are near the center of the racket and not far from each other. The size of this area, which is what most players are really interested in, is greater in racket frames that are stiffer and heavier and have a larger head size.

Strings

The choice of certain tennis racquet strings has long been considered critical by elite players. For the rest of us, the differences in tension, type, and design of racquet stringing may or may not make much of a difference in our play, depending on whom you talk with. In the end, it may come down to a subjective rather than scientific-based decision.

String Composition

Players can choose from natural gut, polyester solid core, solid core single wrap, single core multiple wrap, multifilament core with either single or double wrap, composite, or a hybrid. Gut is more lively and resilient than synthetic strings, has more power and control, holds its tension longer, and provides less shock to the arms. The disadvantage of gut strings is that they are much more expensive. Most players have gone to some kind of synthetic string; however, no synthetic string actually matches the combined advantages of natural gut. The most popular synthetic strings generally comprise a core of nylon or polyester and a wrapping of synthetic filaments that protect the core and thus extend the durability of the string. No string is perfect. Players usually have to select strings based on a tradeoff between factors such as durability, power, vibration, and control.

Players must consider the thickness of the string as well. Thickness ranges from 13 gauge (1.65-1.80 millimeters) to 22 gauge (.60-.70 millimeter). The thinner the strings, the faster the ball comes off the face of the racket. Thin strings also allow a player to put more spin on the ball. The downside is that they break sooner. A thicker string lasts longer and provides more control but delivers less power than a thinner string. Most people compromise and usually select 16 gauge (1.26-1.34 millimeters) strings.

String Tension

The traditional wisdom among tennis players is that the lower the string tension, the greater the power that the racket can deliver to the ball. It may be that because the strings bend more on impact with the ball, a trampolining effect slings the ball back faster. On the other hand, a tightly strung racket, which has more tension, is supposed to provide better control of shots, which means the ball is more likely to head in the intended direction. It's been suggested by tennis physicists that with stiffer strings a greater flattening of the ball occurs, which causes the surface of the ball to get more embedded in the strings. Those who read the research may not be so convinced that the traditional idea of power versus control relative to string tension is all that important. Most research does show that a racket strung more loosely (to a certain point) delivers more power, but the amount of the extra power is very small —maybe just 2 percent or so. Also, uncertainty exists about whether control is really greater with tighter stringing; that's much harder to study in a laboratory. Most of the reports of power versus control relative to stringing tension are subjective and come from players out on the court who say that they can definitely feel the differences.

In a fascinating study, Australian researchers R. Bower and R. Cross examined how well players could actually tell the difference in string tension based on the way a racket played. The researchers asked 41 experienced recreational players whether they could tell the difference in tension of several identical rackets strung at tensions ranging from 40 to 62 pounds per square inch when striking balls fed by a ball machine on a grass court. They found that 73 percent of the players could not discriminate between a racket strung with a tension of 51 pounds and one strung at 62 pounds, and 37 percent were not able to detect a difference of 20 pounds. What's more, this ability to tell the difference in string tension decreased significantly when the participants wore ear plugs so that they could not hear the sound the ball striking the racket. The authors concluded that "77 percent of the players discriminated tension primarily on the basis of impact sound and the other 23 percent discriminated primarily on the basis of racket feel or performance."[2] Based on these findings, how tightly a player strings a racket may not be as important as one might think. These same investigators commented that these results may surprise players who are particular about their string tension.

It should be noted that the conclusions of the study focus on whether recreational players could tell the difference in string tension, not whether the string tension affected playing style. Recreational players may not have a sensitive feeling for their rackets. A study involving professionals may shed additional light on whether changes in string tension are noticeable to elite players.

Stringing tension ranges from about 50 pounds at the lower end to 70 pounds at the upper end. The preferences of the pros vary when it comes to stringing tension. Pete Sampras and Björn Borg strung their sticks at high tensions, such as 75 or 85 pounds, whereas John McEnroe preferred a low tension of around 45 pounds.

String Design

Rackets can be strung in a dense pattern with 18 main strings and 20 cross-strings or in an open pattern with 16 main strings and 18 cross-strings. With the dense pattern, the strings will not bend as much when the player strikes the ball. This means that if an open-pattern racket and a dense-pattern racket are strung with the same tension, the racket with the dense pattern will provide more control but less power. With the dense pattern, the strings last longer before breaking. However, it's more difficult to put topspin on a ball with a dense pattern. With an open pattern it's just the opposite: more power, less control, better-applied topspin, and less durability.

Grip

If there weren't enough choices to make in selecting the optimal racquet, there's still the matter of the composition and size of the grip. Here's what the experts say.

Grip Size

Grip size is usually between 4 1/8 and 4 5/8 inches. In *Bollettieri's Tennis Handbook*, Nick Bollettieri describes how to determine whether the grip is the right size.

> The best way to determine your correct size is to hold the racket comfortably in your playing hand. Turn the racket over to expose your palm and fingertips. You should be able to place the pinkie finger from your free hand comfortably between the heel of your palm and the ring finger of the hand holding the racket. You should have enough room to just touch each.[1]

Bollettieri goes on to point out that players should select a grip size that is on the bigger side rather than the smaller size because a large grip generally allows better control. Because more of the hand is on the handle of a racket with a larger grip, the racket resists twisting when the ball is struck off center. Some have also suggested that a bigger handle better prevents the formation of blisters. Players can increase grip size by applying what are called overgrips, either sticky or dry.

Grip Materials

Players need to select a type of grip as well. Old-style leather grips absorb sweat well and last a long time. Some players don't like these grips because they feel less soft and comfortable. Others feel that leather grips allow more shock to the arm and a greater chance of developing blisters on the hand. Grips made from synthetic materials, on the other hand, are more comfortable and much less expensive than leather grips. However, they can get slippery because they don't absorb sweat as well and they don't last as long as leather grips.

There's a lot to consider when choosing a racket. A player should select a racket with features that are appropriate for his particular style of play. But how much, the inquiring player asks, do these features really influence the play of the average recreational player? That's a matter of opinion. Jack Groppel, in *High Tech Tennis*, cites veteran coach Vic Braden as saying, "It doesn't matter what equipment you use; it's all engineered way beyond your physical capabilities."[6] Perhaps in the end, the best—very unscientific—advice is to simply try out a few rackets and pick one that just *feels* right.

Court Surfaces

It's difficult to think of another sport in which participants are forced to adapt to different playing surfaces. Yet a lifetime tennis player over the age of 60 has probably competed on grass, red clay, concrete, wood, asphalt, cement, green clay (Har-Tru), and acrylic paint. All of these surfaces affect the bounce of the ball and the way players run after it in a different way. This is remarkable considering that the very essence of the game involves an incredibly fine neuromuscular tuning that makes the racket meet the ball at just the right time and place.

Today, most recreational players play on hard courts, clay courts, or maybe even grass courts. How one approaches the game is very different on each of these surfaces. The basic issue is one of friction, which affects how the ball bites into the court surface and how a player might stride to move into the best position to return the ball. Adapting to each surface is an important key to playing success. A player needs to anticipate how the ball is going to bounce as he steps onto the court.

Hard Courts

Hard courts are usually made of acrylic paint mixed with sand that is applied over a base of asphalt or concrete. A layer of rubber, which makes the surface kinder to the legs, is sometimes placed between these two. Not a lot of friction exists between the ball and the hard surface, so the bounce is quick and the ball moves rapidly. As a result, hard courts place big demands on a player's reactions and ability to move fast on the court.

However, hard surfaces create a high-friction effect on the soles of tennis shoes. There's little give as a player changes position. This could be expected to put more strain on the leg muscles as the player suddenly races to track down a lob or dive for a down-the line shot as she approaches the net. That could predispose the player to acute muscle strain or, in the long term, chronic overuse injury.

Hard courts are fitting to those who survive on an aggressive serve-and-volley style of game. Many players, such as John McEnroe, found tennis success by striking sharply angled, low-bouncing shots that sped off the court and provided little time for an opponent to react.

Clay Courts

Clay courts are usually not made of clay but rather some kind of crushed stone. A number of varieties exist. The *terre battue* at the French Open is called red clay because its surface is covered with ochre-colored crushed brick. Green clay, or Har-Tru, a common clay surface in the United States, is covered with crushed basalt rather than brick. The red clay of Roland Garros plays a bit slower than green clay in the United States.

Around the world one can find other variants: maroon clay, yellow clay, and gray clay (the real thing).

The grit of the surface creates greater friction with the ball, which slows the ball down and makes it bounce higher when it strikes the court. The pace of the game on clay is also slowed because the ball arrives at a slower velocity. Howard Brody and colleagues estimated that about 25 percent of the speed of an outgoing ball is determined by the speed at which it comes to the racket.[3] If the ball is slower coming in and slower going out, the tempo of the game is slowed.

On clay, a player has more time to get to the drop shot and more time to set up for a return down the line. Players need more patience with the game on clay courts compared with hard and grass courts. And because the duration of games and rallies on clay is longer, competition on clay demands higher levels of endurance fitness.

Hitting winners is tougher on this surface because the ball bounces more slowly. The opponent has a much easier time getting to the ball and setting up a return shot. This is one reason why players who specialize in a serve-and-volley game generally don't do well on this surface. Clay favors those with a staunch defense who stick to the baseline and hammer away powerful ground strokes. With modern rackets, players can keep opponents off guard with heavy topspin, which is more effective on the clay surface.

Because less friction exists between shoes and the court surface on clay, a player can effectively slide into shots—a talent honed by professionals who excel on this surface. Controversy exists about whether the construction of the sole of a particular tennis shoe influences its action on clay. However, those who play on this surface most of the time might find it worthwhile to carefully look at the manufacturer's claims regarding a shoe's suitability for playing on clay when selecting a pair.

One might expect the lower friction and greater resilience of clay to lessen the impact on the lower extremities. In a study by Jean-Bernard Fabre and colleagues in France, 10 experienced tennis players competed in a three-hour singles match alternatively on indoor hard and clay courts.[5] The researchers measured forces of muscle contraction and leg muscle electrical activation (electromyography). It turned out that, as expected, fatigue was evident after the competitions: Forces of muscle contraction declined by about 5 to 10 percent. Interestingly, no differences were found in this fatigue effect when playing on the two surfaces. That seems to be unexpected because clay is supposed to be easier on the legs. If the competition on the clay had been longer (as would be typical) in this study, maybe some differences would have been evident. Traditionally, it has always been considered that players exhibit earlier fatigue and greater predisposition to injury on clay because competition on this surface requires more strokes and longer duration of play than competition on hard or grass courts does.

Grass Courts

Modern tennis originated on grass courts, and grass it remains at Wimbledon. Grass is a fast surface because, unlike on clay courts, there is no grit to cause friction on the ball. Grass courts are generally even faster than most hard courts because the ball often skids off the slippery surface. This makes balls bounce low. Like hard courts, this surface is more to the liking of the serve-and-volley specialist, who can fire angled, fast-moving winning shots from the forecourt.

Although both hard and grass courts are fast, differences in style of play do exist between the two. M. Hughes and S. Clark at the Sports Performance Institute at the University of Technology in Auckland, New Zealand, used video to analyze the effect of grass and synthetic hard surfaces on play at Wimbledon and the Australian championships, respectively, in 1992.[7] They found that the average number of shots in a rally was markedly greater (by 52 percent) on the hard courts than on the grass courts and that the average time for each rally was 93 percent greater on the hard court. On grass, the points are quicker due to the faster speed of the ball.

Grass courts, like those at Wimbledon, are generally fast and make balls bounce low, which is best suited for a skilled serve-and-volley player like Pete Sampras.

Glyn Kirk/Action Plus/Icon SMI

Line Calls

Consider for a moment the factors that go into winning or losing on the tennis court: player skill, the opponent's abilities, the capacity of a coach to motivate, playing environment, weather, and the judgment of umpires or referees. The player has control over only the first of these. This has been a message traditionally used by sport psychologists: Just do your best because that's all you can do. Whether a player wins or loses otherwise is determined by other factors.

There is no question that making accurate line calls in tennis can be a difficult task. Consider what a player is trying to do here: The ball is arriving at a rapid velocity. If it is John Isner's first serve, the ball is coming at the player at a speed of about 200 feet (61 m) each second. This means that when the ball strikes the court—when the player has to decide whether it is in or out—it will cover a foot (.3 m) in 5 milliseconds. The player can't actually sense the ball striking the court, so his judgment of where it struck is based on its abrupt change in direction. The player tries to identify the point of contact— where the trajectory of the ball suddenly rises—while his primary mental focus is directed toward returning the ball while in motion.

Most research on this subject has focused on the accuracy of calls made by professional tennis referees. The task of making a call is different for referees than for players. Referees do not have to track the ball in flight; rather, they simply stare fixedly at the line in question. Referees are not moving and do not have any emotional stake in whether the ball is in or out. However, much of the information that comes from this research may have bearing on how players make close line calls in a recreational or club tennis setting.

Tennis referees are very good at what they do. Even with the most powerful serve they can usually estimate the landing spot of the ball within a few centimeters. Still, as is known from video replay technology, they do make mistakes. George Mather, a psychologist at the University of Sussex, analyzed line calls in professional tennis play to define the perceptual limits of line judges.[9] He estimated that about 8 percent of all line calls involving balls landing within 100 millimeters of a line are not called correctly.

Studies in the laboratory setting have indicated that people commonly perceive moving objects as being displaced forward in the direction of motion. This explains why referees are more likely to erroneously call a ball out (or long) when it actually hit the line than to mistakenly call the ball in. For example,

David Whitney and colleagues at the University of California, Davis analyzed a total of more than 4,000 points recorded during Wimbledon play. Video replay indicated that, of 83 points that were called erroneously, 70 were wrongly called out when the ball was shifted in the direction of motion and 13 were erroneously called in.[11]

Because tennis championships can ride on a millimeter here and there and because player skill and power are increasing, the demand for video replay technology to reduce the human error inherent in line calls was inevitable. Since 2006, the Hawk-Eye system has been regularly incorporated in the judging of major professional tennis events. This system allows players to challenge what they consider inaccurate line calls by human line judges. Players are limited to three incorrect challenges per set, and the process of displaying the shot and its landing point in reference to the line is performed expeditiously in order to minimize the disruption to the flow of play. Although most players have embraced the advantages of this system, some still remain skeptical of its accuracy.

Multiple video cameras track the ball from various angles on the court. The accumulated two-dimensional images of the flight path of the ball are electronically converted into a three-dimensional track, and the oval-shaped strike point (from ball compression and skid) is clearly displayed to determine the accuracy of the judge's call on court. These cameras operate at a very high frame rate (~500 frames per second), so the strike point can be accurately identified and displayed. The average limit of accuracy of this system is reportedly 3.6 millimeters. The diameter of a tennis ball, for comparison, is 67 millimeters.

This system dramatically reduces the number of inaccurate line calls, but there is still no way to get it perfect. Harry Collins and Robert Evans of the school of social sciences at Cardiff University in the United Kingdom published an interesting analysis of the uncertainties of the Hawk-Eye system.[4] They are concerned that the graphics of the Hawk-Eye system impose an unrealistic sense of accuracy, leaving the viewer with a false idea of its precision. According to these authors, the accuracy of the system (established by very-high-speed cameras) was accepted by the International Tennis Federation after finding that the maximum discrepancy between the distance of the impact from the line and the true distance was 10 millimeters. Collins and Evans comment:

> In real life, the edge of a line painted on grass cannot be defined to an accuracy of one millimeter. First because grass and paint are not like that, and second, because even given perfect paint and perfect surface to draw on, the apparatus used to paint the line is unlikely to maintain its accuracy to one millimeter over the width of the court. Furthermore, tennis balls are furry and it is not clear that their edges can be defined to an accuracy of one millimeter.[4]

It seems that no matter how hard referees and players try, there will always be times when they are confronted with doubt. In making line calls, even this sophisticated video replay system leaves room for uncertainty.

CHAPTER 8

The Trained Tennis Body

A player can practice extensively, perfect a deadly backhand slice, develop a cannonball serve, and devise ingenious court strategies, but when he gets tired it all goes out the window. Mental concentration weakens, timing goes, footwork gets lazy, and court speed slows. Fatigue means a deterioration of performance, often at the most crucial juncture of the match—that critical third set when a player needs to give the very best.

A player's ability to withstand the effects of fatigue can mean the difference between victory and defeat, even when up against a supposedly more talented opponent. If the opponent across the net tires first, the opponent's nifty slice and kicking second serve are going to be of no avail. Improving fitness, defined here as the characteristic of avoiding or delaying fatigue, should be a top priority for the competitive tennis player. In a setting where everybody has technical ability, resistance to fatigue in long matches can keep one at the top of the rankings. The pros have learned this; it holds for the recreational player as well.

In one of the most astounding tennis events in recent memory, John Isner and Nicolas Mahut survived an epic 11-hour battle at Wimbledon in 2010. It was the longest match in tennis history. It lasted so long because neither could break the serve of the other: Isner had 112 service aces and Mahut had 103 (the previous record was 78). Isner eventually won, 70-68, in the fifth-set tie breaker. "I'm tired watching this," quipped television announcer John McEnroe.

This chapter examines the causes of fatigue during tennis play and the mechanisms by which fatigue occurs. It also considers methods that might help players resist fatigue and thereby prevent the deterioration of performance in long, tight matches.

John Isner and Nicolas Mahut pose next to the scoreboard at Wimbledon after their dramatic, record-setting 11-hour match.

Antoine Couvercelle/Tennis Magazine/DPPI/Icon SMI

Physical Demands of Tennis

Sport scientists have demonstrated the detrimental effects of fatigue during extended tennis play. After about an hour of tennis play, hitting inaccuracy, unforced errors, and mental mistakes begin to creep in; serve and stroke velocity decline; and speed of running to the ball decreases. Oliver Girard and colleagues of the faculty of sport science at the University of Montpelier examined the maximal force of leg contraction, leg stiffness, jumping height, and muscle soreness in 12 well-trained tennis players before, after, and every 30 minutes during a 3-hour competitive match.[6] Leg force declined by almost 10 percent during play. Jumping ability stayed stable during play but declined 30 minutes afterward. Both muscle soreness and rating of perceived exertion (i.e., how tired the players felt) increased progressively during the match.

Interestingly, studies on the effect of prolonged tennis play (or simulated conditions) on performance have not always been consistent, and some case findings have been inexplicably conflicting. In one study, for instance, fatigue reduced accuracy of tennis strokes by as much as 81 percent. In a review of this subject, however, Daniel Hornery and colleagues at the Australian Institute of Sport in Canberra concluded that "under physiological strain, stroke accuracy is largely maintained whereas stroke velocity is more likely to deteriorate".[8] Some authors have found very minimal effects of fatigue on tennis performance. Hornery and colleagues suggested that such discrepancies might reflect the methodological limitations of these studies, including inadequate assessment of the multifaceted skills involved in tennis that contribute to performance, the use of nontennis interventions to cause fatigue, and levels of fatigue that did not simulate those expected to occur in real match play.

Nevertheless, the physical demands of tennis can be extreme, especially at the professional level. In a 6-hour slugfest —the longest final in the 107-year history of the Australian Open—Novak Djokovic came out on top 5-7, 6-4, 6-2, 6-7(5) 7-5 over Rafael Nadal. Both players were near collapse at the final point. "I'll never forget this match," said Nadal afterward.

If players want to learn techniques for preventing deterioration of performance due to fatigue, they must first understand what causes fatigue in the first place. Researchers have carefully analyzed the characteristics of a typical tennis match at high levels of competition.

- During a tennis match, the time spent actually playing is approximately 20 to 30 percent greater on clay courts than on faster court surfaces.
- Play is intermittent and consists of work periods of 5 to 10 seconds. These periods are interrupted by 10 to 20 seconds of rest and by pauses of 60 to 90 seconds during court changeovers.
- On average, each player strikes the ball 2 to 3 times per rally.

- From the ready position, 80 percent of balls are struck within 2.5 meters. The player moves 2.5 to 4.5 meters in approximately 10 percent of strokes and more than 4.5 meters in 5 percent of strokes.
- In the course of a point, a player runs an average of 8 to 12 meters and changes directions 3 to 5 times.
- Serves account for 12 to 18 percent of total strokes during service games.
- A serve-and-volley player moves forward 20 to 40 percent more than does a baseline player, who moves laterally 60 to 80 percent of the time.

Sources: Mendez-Villanueva et al.,[13]; Johnson and McHugh[9]; Roetert and Kovacs[18]; Groppel and Roetert[7].

Tennis is a game of repetitive short, high-intensity sprints that often require explosive strength (i.e., quick steps and leg push-off) along with muscular force at the shoulder and upper extremity when striking the ball. These are coupled with the need for a high degree of mental focus, visuomotor timing, and attention to visual tracking. The player must repeat all of these activities over the course of about two hours (or sometimes five hours or even more in professional play). Also, in some tournament settings players may be called on to compete in successive matches with limited time for rest and recuperation.

Mechanisms of Fatigue

Now that we have characterized the types of work necessary to play tennis, we can examine the factors that might contribute to tennis-related fatigue. Despite many decades of solid research, exercise scientists have not yet pinpointed the principal mechanism that explains exercise fatigue. What is clear, though, is that there are a number of prime candidates for this cause of fatigue within the chain of events that encompass muscular performance during physical activity, including limitations in oxygen supply to muscles, critical diminution of glycogen, and a decline in neurological stimulation. Let's now examine a number of these potential determinants in order to try to formulate an opinion regarding which might be most critical to the cause of fatigue during tennis competition.

Energy Deficit

Mechanisms of energy supply can play a role in influencing physical fitness. Limitations of such energy availability might affect fatigue threshold during tennis play. In order to deliver a devastating half-court volley, a player's muscles must have a source of energy. The most immediate source of that energy in the muscle cell is the compound adenosine triphosphate (ATP). Without this energy, muscle contraction cannot occur.

Muscle cells normally contain a small amount of ATP—just enough energy to provide for brief bursts of activity that last less than a few seconds. Actions such as stealing a base, an off-tackle run, and a tennis swing are accomplished largely via the energy stored in this supply of ATP. However, after this burst of activity the ATP is used up and must be replenished before either repeated short bursts of physical activity or more extended exercise can be accomplished.

This replenishment can occur by two mechanisms. For short-burst activities of no more than a minute or two, the ATP supply is mainly refurbished by anaerobic metabolism, called such because this process does not utilize oxygen in its biochemical pathways (called glycolysis). During a short sprint that lasts five to six seconds, about one half of the energy is derived from stored ATP and the remaining half is derived from anaerobic metabolism.

For more extended endurance activities such as distance running or cycling, ATP is replenished continuously through aerobic metabolism. This involves a series of biochemical steps that require a supply of oxygen, which is provided via the lungs and circulatory system. The efficiency of this mechanism is often referred to as one's cardiovascular fitness because capacity for aerobic metabolism is directly related to performance on endurance events that necessitate top function of the heart and lungs.

In reality, the performance of a given form of exercise does not rely on just one of these mechanisms. Rather, a continuum exists between the relative contributions of ATP stores and its replenishment by anaerobic and aerobic metabolism. For example, in track and field the 100-meter event is predominantly fueled by pre-existing ATP stores and anaerobic glycolysis. As events become longer (e.g., 200 meter, 400 meter, 5,000 meter), the relative contribution of aerobic metabolism increases. The percentage of energy supplied by anaerobic metabolism increases as events last more than 10 seconds but declines when the event lasts more than about three minutes.

Training programs are designed to improve anaerobic or aerobic fitness by mimicking the activity in which the athlete participates. Marathon runners are not often found in the weight room. Sprinters do not spend Sunday mornings on 20-kilometer mountain runs. In the present analysis of tennis, then, it is important to assess the extent to which the different energy-providing mechanisms contribute to the sport. This can help identify training regimens that are pertinent to improving fitness in tennis.

Stored ATP and Anaerobic Fitness

Tennis is a stop-and-go game of short (5-10 second) bursts of high-intensity exercise interspersed with brief periods of rest. From the metabolic patterns outlined previously, one would expect that tennis exercise is supported by energy derived from stored ATP and anaerobic metabolism. However, serum lactate levels, which are a general indicator of the extent of anaerobic metabolism, are not found to be significantly increased during tennis play. This led exercise scientists Tom Reilly and John Palmer at John Moores University in Liverpool to conclude, perhaps surprisingly, that "anaerobic glycolysis does not play a major role in metabolism during tennis play."[17]

Restoration of ATP stores after vigorous exercise from anaerobic sources may take as long as three to five minutes, and with the short rest periods between points in tennis, recovery is incomplete. That would lead to fatigue on the next point. It has been suggested that the cardiovascular system makes up for this deficit by including energy derived from aerobic metabolism.

Some experimental data support this idea. German researchers Alexander Ferrauti and colleagues in the faculty of sport science at Ruhr-Universität Bochum demonstrated that running speed and quality of tennis strokes deteriorated during drills as recovery time between exercise bouts decreased.[4] Adequate replacement of energy (ATP) is dependent on rest periods between points on the tennis court. Players should take their time between points in order to give the aerobic metabolism some time to build up sufficient ATP before the next serve.

Aerobic Fitness

At first impression, aerobic fitness might not be considered important for tennis players, whose sport largely consists of a series of brief sprints, strength, and accuracy in striking the ball. However, considerable evidence shows that the aerobic-energy mechanism does play an important role in this sport and that, consequently, aerobic training should be a part of each player's regimen.

As noted previously, aerobically derived energy for endurance exercise requires oxygen, so one can estimate the contribution of aerobic fitness involved in tennis by measuring the amount of oxygen consumed during play. One can also determine a player's maximal oxygen uptake (called $\dot{V}O_2max$) on a treadmill or cycle test in the exercise laboratory in order to assess the level of aerobic fitness.

The $\dot{V}O_2max$ of high-level male tennis players has generally been reported to be between 55 and 60 milliliters per kilogram per minute. To put this into perspective, the average $\dot{V}O_2max$ in the general nonathletic population of young adult males is 35 to 45 milliliters per kilogram per minute, whereas that of an Olympic marathon champion can be expected to be about 80 milliliters per kilogram per minute. This finding suggests that aerobic mechanisms play a role—but not a predominant one—in tennis play.

Oxygen uptake ($\dot{V}O_2$) has been measured during actual tennis competition. The best study was performed by Gerhard Smekal and colleagues at the Institute of Sport Sciences at the

University of Vienna, who used portable monitoring equipment to determine $\dot{V}O_2$ during 10 50-minute singles matches in elite Austrian players.[19] $\dot{V}O_2$max for this group on a treadmill test averaged 57 milliliters per kilogram per minute. During a singles game, $\dot{V}O_2$ varied from 10.4 to 47.8 milliliters per kilogram per minute; the average was 29.1 milliliters per kilogram per minute (51 percent of $\dot{V}O_2$max). This is approximately the value that one would expect while taking a brisk walk around the neighborhood. The authors concluded from these data that the average energy demands of tennis from aerobic metabolism were rather low. Importantly, the style of play in this investigation affected aerobic energy expenditure. The average $\dot{V}O_2$ when two defensive-minded players were competing was higher than when two offense-minded players were competing (30.8 vs. 27.5 milliliters per kilogram per minute).

The reason for the increased $\dot{V}O_2$ in tennis play likely lies in the need for aerobic metabolism to replenish ATP between points. That's probably why players find themselves panting between tough points. The increased ventilation supplies more oxygen to the muscle cells in the aerobic process of replacing the ATP that was used up as the player tried to run down that angled shot to the corner.

In the process of aerobic metabolism, energy is supplied to build ATP stores when the oxygen arriving at the muscle cell chemically reacts (i.e., burns) with stored glycogen. Glycogen is formed from the ingestion by an individual of glucose and other sugars. Glycogen, then, is like the gasoline in a car, which mixes with air and burns via the spark plugs to drive the cylinders. Extended endurance exercise depletes this glycogen supply. Many feel that this exhaustion of glycogen is the limiting factor—the cause of fatigue—in distance events such as the marathon.

It makes intuitive sense, then, that extra glucose supplied to the body during extended periods of exercise would enhance performance. A number of studies involving time-trial performance in highly trained cyclists have demonstrated just this. During prolonged pedaling events that last two to three hours, oral consumption of glucose has improved endurance times by as much as 33 percent. No clear evidence suggests that a similar glucose supplementation would delay fatigue during tennis play because experimental information is insufficient to answer the question. Tennis involves repeated bouts of short-burst activity. Each point usually lasts no more than 10 seconds, and players take rest periods for recovery between points. The challenge of tennis is very different than that of a three-hour continuous-cycle time trial at high exercise intensities. No one has ever documented a decrease in blood sugar levels during competitive tennis play—at least in competition lasting up to three hours. The very modest increase in $\dot{V}O_2$ that occurs during tennis play suggests that glycogen supply would not be exhausted even during prolonged competition.

On the other hand, the findings of an investigation by Belgian exercise scientists Lieven Vergauwen and colleagues are interesting.[21] This group studied the effect of a carbohydrate (sugar-containing) drink with and without caffeine during the Leuven Tennis Performance Test in 13 well-trained tennis players. This measure evaluated stroke quality by determining error rate, ball velocity, and precision of ball placement during actual court play (4 games of 10 rallies each) in response to balls delivered by a machine. They found that after players ingested a placebo (containing neither carbohydrate nor caffeine) stroke quality deteriorated as play progressed; however, this decline was attenuated after the players ingested carbohydrate. No separate effect of caffeine was observed. These authors concluded that ingestion of carbohydrate during competition may improve the quality of strokes during extended tennis play.

Neuromuscular Factors

Explosive muscle strength and speed are critical for effective tennis play. Initial acceleration toward the ball, power generated in delivering a serve, and ability to rapidly change direction are all key elements of the game. How fast a player can set up for the next shot, how many steps he takes to get there, and the velocity of his strokes are all important in winning each point.

These features are all dependent on the functional capacity and number of nerves that trigger the muscle fibers to contract. The process begins in the brain (which either consciously or unconsciously directs muscular action) and ends in nerve fiber endings in individual muscle fibers. Along the way, numerous connections in this electrical wiring pattern may be susceptible to fatigue during repeated bouts of exercise. Here, then, is perhaps a better explanation for fatigue that accompanies tennis play. Maybe when you get tired on the court it's really effectively a muscular electrical failure. By this explanation, the force and speed of muscular contractions decline as these electrical connections weaken with extended time on the court. A player tires because the electrical drive for muscle contraction is diminished. Some good experimental data back up this idea.

Researchers have demonstrated that neural drive to muscle cells progressively declines in the performance of repeated intermittent exercise, as is typical of tennis play. This could have several consequences. For instance, as might be expected from common experience, finish times steadily decline as an athlete repeatedly performs sprints. Ari Nummela and colleagues at the Research Institute for Olympic Sports in Jyväskylä, Finland, measured performance after participants had completed 400-meter runs and found a 13 percent decline in leg muscle force and a 19 percent decline in running speed.[14]

Translated to tennis play, that means that a player can expect to get to the ball slower as a match continues. Like a sprinter getting off the blocks at the sound of the starter's gun, the first steps taken during tennis play are critical, and with repeated sprinting activity this initial acceleration decreases. This is probably related to a decline in both strength and speed of muscle contraction as a manifestation of diminished neural innervation.

Players also have to be able to react rapidly. The rate of force development—just how quickly a nerve can fire a muscle to contract—is critical to tennis play. It is well-recognized that the rate of force development created by a muscle is linked to neural drive. It's likely, then, that the rate of force development decreases gradually over the course of a vigorous match, causing the players to react slower.

Explosive strength, reaction time, court speed, shot accuracy, and racket head speed can all be impeded by a progressive deterioration in neural drive to muscles during the course of tennis competition. Just why the electrical activation of muscles might decline as nerve action decreases with repeated exercise is not clear. It could be that the amount of chemical agents (neurotransmitters) that permit electricity to cross the gap (synapse) between nerve fibers or nerve endings and muscle cells declines or that the electrical process itself, caused by sodium and potassium ions crossing in and out of nerve cell membranes, is diminished. The problem might be in the muscle cell itself, where the arriving electrical impulse is supposed to trigger entry of calcium ions into the contractile apparatus but maybe gets tired of doing so. Or maybe centers in the brain that are charged with initiating the electrical signal to cause the muscles to contract wear down. Perhaps the decreased ability to concentrate and increasing number of mental mistakes that occur with prolonged play can be traced to a similar occurrence of chemical fatigue in the brain. By whatever process, it is likely that a decline in neuromuscular drive is a prominent determinant of fatigue during intermittent short bursts of vigorous exercise that are typical of tennis play.

Heat

Most people tire more easily during exercise performed in the heat, and most players know from playing on sweltering summer afternoons that their tennis games deteriorate rapidly in hot court conditions. Researchers have documented this quite nicely. At the University of Aberdeen in Scotland, physiologists Stuart Galloway and Ron Maughan reported that adult cyclists could pedal for an average of 93 minutes in temperatures of 11 degrees Celsius, 80 minutes in 21 degrees Celsius, and only 50 minutes in 31 degrees Celsius before fatigue set in.[5] Why is exercise tolerance is so markedly limited in hot environmental conditions?

The traditional explanation has been linked to cardiovascular stress. Muscles become warm during exercise because muscle contraction is only about 25 percent efficient; that is, 25 percent goes into moving the body and the remaining 75 percent is released as heat. That heat has to be eliminated. The thermoregulatory functions of the body get rid of work-produced heat in the muscles by transmitting it via the circulatory system to the skin, where it is released into the air by the process of convection. It then instigates sweating to cool the body by evaporation.

Hot environmental conditions challenge both of these mechanisms. The amount of heat released by convection is directly related to the difference between skin temperature and the temperature of the surrounding air. When it is warmer outside, the gradient is diminished and heat loss is less. That puts more responsibility for heat loss on sweat evaporation, which can be limited in hot climatic conditions, particularly when the relative humidity is high. The result, then, is that body temperature increases faster when exercising in the heat.

Players become more fatigued in this condition because circulatory blood flow to the exercising muscles is insufficient. This occurs for two reasons. First, increased blood flow must go to the skin to release heat, leaving less to supply the muscle. Second, body fluid content and blood volume are decreased with increased sweating. As a result, the blood supply and oxygen remaining for muscular contraction are diminished.

There remains no question that dehydration during exercise in the heat, which occurs as a result of water loss through sweat, increases the rate of increase in core body temperature and induces early fatigue. Most studies have suggested that decrements of performance in many sports can occur with a body fluid loss of as little as 2 percent. This level of dehydration is commonly reported in tennis players during extended play in hot climatic conditions.

Meir Magal and colleagues at the University of Southern Mississippi examined the effects of dehydration during a 75-

minute tennis match on tennis performance in 11 experienced adult male tennis players (USTA ranking 4.0-5.0). Ambient temperature ranged from 29 degrees Celsius to 38 degrees Celsius.[12] Body weight decreased by an average of 2.7 percent, which was accompanied by deterioration in 5-meter and 10-meter sprint times. Agility, groundstroke, and serve performance, however, were not affected. In this study, heat most negatively affected speed.

Early fatigue and depression of performance in the heat may occur via several mechanisms. Dehydration from sweating lowers blood supply to muscles. This effect may be exacerbated by blood supply from the central circulation flowing to the skin for cooling. Many, such as L. Nybo and colleagues at the August Krogh Institute in Copenhagen, believe that fatigue with exercise in the heat is principally an expression of the brain's reaction to the body reaching a critical temperature (above which one would be at risk for heat stroke as well as mental and cardiac dysfunction).[15] This limiting governor acts as a protective mechanism, causing sensations of fatigue and decreased central command to muscle that make the individual stop exercising.

How hot do tennis players get when playing in the heat? Information is limited. Exercise physiologist Michael Bergeron and colleagues at the Medical College of Georgia measured core temperatures in 11 young males playing outside in the National Boys' 14 Tournament in San Antonio, Texas.[1] The wet-bulb globe temperature at the time averaged 29.6 degrees Celsius, which is considered a high-risk level of temperature. Core temperature was measured with an ingested monitor pill, and fluid consumption was permitted ad libitum. After a full singles match, body weight decreased by an average of .9 percent and core temperature increased from 37.7 degrees Celsius to 38.6 degrees Celsius. The limited increase in core temperature in this rather extreme setting may have been tempered by the fluid intake, which prevented significant dehydration, and the fact that "all eight singles matches were fairly easy straight set win (two sets only), with only one set going to a tie break."[1]

In a similar study, Bergeron and colleagues found an increase in core temperature averaging +.9 degrees Celsius in adolescent tennis players who completed two 120-minute training sessions in a warm environment (79 degrees Fahrenheit; 26.1 degrees Celsius). Again with ad libitum drinking, dehydration amounted to a loss of only .9 percent of body weight. Exercise physiologist Melissa Tippet and the research team at the Gatorade Sports Science Institute reported similar findings.[20] They measured core temperature during match play in seven professional female tennis players competing in a hot environment (wet bulb temperature approximately 30 degrees Celsius) with ad libitum fluid intake. Average core temperature increased from 37.8 degrees Celsius prematch to 38.9 degrees Celsius at the end of the match, and loss of body mass was 1.2 percent.

These studies reveal that in a setting of ad libitum fluid intake no serious increase in thermal strain occurs during singles competition of modest duration, even when played in hot environmental conditions. Ad libitum fluid intake by tennis players can be sufficient to prevent significant dehydration—and, presumably, deterioration of performance. More research information on the effect of hydration practices and levels and frequency of competition on dehydration and fatigue during tennis play is clearly needed.

Of additional concern, however, is the effect on hydration and thermal status when competitive matches are played back to back without adequate time for rest, hydration, and recuperation. Although such situations do not generally arise at the top professional level, lower-level tournaments frequently are constructed such that serial matches are unavoidable. Dehydration can accumulate in such situations and potentially lead to diminished performance as well as possible hyperthermia that could pose a risk of heat injury, such as heat stroke or syncope.

John Coyle of the Heart Center of Tulsa studied 370 competitors who played repeated singles matches on the same day during the United States Tennis Association 14's National Hard Court Championships, which are played in San Antonio during the first two weeks of August.[3] The average wet bulb temperature was 31.9 degrees Celsius. Coyle found that the outcome of the second match was directly related to the time duration and temperature level (recorded as heat stress) of the first match. The less the heat stress in the first match, the more likely the player would win in the second. The author concluded that although it could not be determined whether this was a direct effect of the hot environment or reflected some other influence the findings certainly appeared to incriminate fatigue factors and the possibility that cumulative heat stress from an earlier match was detrimental to performance in a second match played not long after.

Mike Bergeron and his research team looked at this issue more directly in an exercise-testing laboratory. In their study, 24 adolescent athletes (mainly soccer) performed two 80-minute exercise bouts on the treadmill and cycle ergometer at a moderate intensity in a hot environment (33 degrees Celsius). The participants rested for one hour in a cool room between bouts. Fluid intake was dictated to prevent significant dehydration. Somewhat surprisingly, the increase in core temperature and heart rate during the second bout of exercise was not significantly different from that during the first. That is, no carryover effects were observed. (What was greater in the second bout, however, was the participants' rating of perceived exertion; they described themselves as feeling more tired, particularly the older participants.) The authors noted that their negative findings might be explained by the fact that all participants were fully hydrated before starting the second bout of exercise and that the environmental conditions (i.e., one full hour rest in a cool room) did not fully mimic repeated play in a tennis tournament:

Moreover the next round of competition is often contested later in the day when it is hotter. Thus, without the same physiological advantages provided by our laboratory protocol, it is reasonable to expect a greater impact of previous strenuous physical activity and heat exposure on subsequent same-day physiological and perceptual strain in the field with a concomitant negative effect on performance.[1]

The research information is far from complete. Nonetheless, certain ideas in the published scientific literature may provide some guidance about the most likely causes of fatigue. Based on this list, it is possible to formulate training regimens that may help delay the decline in performance as players tire in extended matches.

Strategies for Delaying Fatigue

At least five processes may contribute to fatigue during tennis play: depletion of energy substrate, limitations of aerobic fitness (for ATP replenishment), depressed neural drive (from decreased central command, diminished neurotransmitter release, and limited calcium release locally in the muscle fiber), increased core temperature (particularly in hot and humid environmental conditions), and dehydration (from sweat loss along with inadequate fluid replacement). Just how might training practices mitigate these negative influences?

First of all, the research information is far from complete. In fact, given the importance of fatigue in limiting performance in tennis as well as other sports, it's somewhat surprising that more research attention hasn't focused on this issue. Also, studies focusing specifically on fatigue and real-world tennis performance on the court are scant. However, certain approaches to training can be suggested based on possible causes of fatigue in tennis identified in the current scientific literature.

This book is not meant to provide guidance about proper tennis training and competition. That task is left to other authors (e.g., Pluim and Safran[16], Bollettieri[2], Roetert and Kovacs[18]). However, it's fitting to take the information in the previous section and briefly consider how it might indicate ways to lessen fatigue in tennis play and improve performance late in long matches. As many authors have pointed out, improving overall fitness for tennis may also be a valuable means of preventing injuries.

The strategy of training is to take advantage of the body's plasticity of physiological function in order to improve aspects of tennis play that contribute to fatigue. Such training should be focused on elements that are specific to tennis; that is training activities that raise the threshold of fatigue should mimic as closely as possible activities involved in actual tennis play.

As Paul Roetert and Mark Kovacs emphasize, a number of factors dictate how one might construct an antifatigue training program for tennis.[18] Take style of play, for instance. Strong leg muscles, speed, and agility are particularly important for the serve-and-volley specialist, who must bend down to strike low returns and who requires sharp volleying skills. The generation of power through muscle strength is more critical for the aggressive baseliner, who bashes powerful strokes from the back of the court. Emphasis during training on strengthening upper-body muscles will therefore be important. The defensive counterpuncher spends a lot of time running down balls. Therefore, speed and agility should play a prominent role in this player's training regimen.

The type of court surface comes into play as well. On fast courts such as grass, the ball bounces lower and players must bend their knees more when striking the ball. This calls for an emphasis on lunges and squats in strength training. On clay, the ball bounce is slowed by about 15 percent and points (and matches) are longer. Here, work on muscular endurance is more critical.

- **Endurance.** Aerobic metabolism is central to performance in events in which large muscle groups contract regularly over extended periods of time (e.g., distance running or swimming). Although this pattern is not observed in tennis, aerobic fitness is important in some capacity in this sport as a means of replenishing energy availability. This may be particularly important in matches of extended duration. Thus, the tennis player's training regimen should include some form of endurance training.

Some have suggested that tennis players can achieve necessary increases in $\dot{V}O_2$max simply by playing tennis regularly. More specific to improving aerobic fitness, though, is a regimen of regular aerobic exercise (e.g., running, biking, rowing) 2 to 3 times a week for 30 to 40 minutes. This regimen typically increases $\dot{V}O_2$max by 5 to 10 percent in athletes such as tennis players or helps maintain high levels of aerobic fitness in those who already have superior values.

- **Muscle strength and power.** Maintaining grip strength and generating rapid racket-head speed are essential elements of tennis play. All studies that compare expert tennis players with those in the middle of the rankings, players with nonplayers, or dominant arm with nondominant arm in experienced players have demonstrated significantly greater (by as much as 40 percent) grip, leg, and arm strength in the former. Besides contributing to stronger shots and delaying fatigue, greater muscle strength may be important in preventing overuse injuries of the wrist, shoulder, and elbow.

  Resistance training is thus a critical part of the tennis player's training regimen. Single maximal lifts increase strength, whereas exercises using lower loads improve muscle endurance; both are important issues for competitive tennis players. Exercises that emphasize rapid development of muscle power are important in the development of explosive strength, which players need in order to accelerate and decelerate rapidly in response to playing situations. *Tennis Anatomy* by Paul Roetert and Mark Kovacs provides good, practical advice on how such training should focus on muscle groups specific not just to tennis play but to particular strokes as well.[18]

- **Speed.** Short-burst, repetitive sprint drills on the court have long been a staple of tennis training. These directly mimic the repeated bursts of high activity, speed getting to the ball, and rapid reaction time that typify the game. As veteran tennis coach Nick Bollettieri has claimed from his years of experience, "This work will help develop the nervous system, 'wiring' the players to be like superfit players who appear to float on top of the court."[2]

- **Agility and flexibility.** Plyometric exercises enhance players' capacity for rapid changes in muscle contraction and develop agility and flexibility. These exercises often involve jumping up onto and down off of boxes, which, although hardly pleasurable, offers significant positive dividends.

- **Thermoregulation.** One cannot control the environmental temperature, but certain measures are useful in mitigating the direct effects of the heat on the court. The body increases tolerance to exercise in the heat as an outcome of repeated bouts of play. This is termed heat acclimation. The more a player plays in the heat, the longer and better he can tolerate it before fatigue sets in. If a player has an important competition coming up that will likely be played in hot conditions, he should do as much as possible to play in such conditions for a week or two before the match. Another aspect that can help is maintaining a high level of aerobic fitness. Those with higher $\dot{V}O_2$max appear to thermoregulate better and demonstrate faster heat acclimation.

  Performance in hot climatic conditions can be aided by maintaining high fitness and allowing time for acclimation before competing in the heat. Players should not forget other common-sense strategies, such as wearing light, loose clothing, keeping in the shade as much as possible, staying hydrated, and donning a cap.

- **Hydration.** Everyone knows that staying well-hydrated during tennis play is important. Sport drink advertisements, coaches, mothers—all remind players to drink. And they're right. Once body fluid content starts to decrease by more than 2 percent of body weight, core temperature begins to shoot up, which causes early fatigue, decreases in performance, and a risk of heat injury (i.e., heat exhaustion and heat stroke). Decreased circulatory flow to muscles may contribute to early fatigue. Keeping well hydrated is one of the most critical factors in the difference between winning and losing, particularly in hot environmental conditions.

A discussion of the important particulars of type, quantity, and timing of drinking fluids during tennis play exceeds the scope of this chapter. The reader is instead referred to Pluim and Safran's review of this subject.[16] A few essential points to emphasize: Arrive at the court fully hydrated, don't drink anything during competitive play that you haven't tried in practice before, and drink some fluids at every opportunity.

- **Energy repletion.** It remains uncertain whether increasing caloric intake during competition—through sport drinks, energy gels, or solid food such as bananas—will delay fatigue in tennis play. From a theoretical standpoint, little evidence supports this idea. Energy utilization during tennis play (i.e., oxygen uptake) is not high, and depletion of glycogen stores even with extended play seems to be unlikely. On the other hand, some research data by Lieven Vergauwen suggest that consuming calories during long matches can sustain stroke skill and accuracy.[21] Some players will surely say, anecdotally, that consuming some food during changeovers helps. Perhaps the best advice here is to follow personal experience. If consuming a banana invigorates you between the second and third sets, it's a good strategy. If such consumption simply loads you down, it's not.

  A wise strategy for maintaining energy stores during tennis play is to normally consume a well-rounded diet that emphasizes carbohydrate. A player who consumes such a diet arrives at the court well stocked up. The same advice goes for postmatch meals. It is important to eat well and properly during recovery to regain any lost energy sources, particularly if you have another match the next day.

In summary, the scientific data have not clearly pinpointed the specific causes of fatigue with tennis play. However, the factors that might contribute to limiting performance are clearly defined, and tennis players can engage in specific training strategies to cover these possible determinants of fatigue on the court.[10,11] Training regimens can be tailored to the specific strengths and weaknesses of the individual player in order to optimize interventions to improve fitness on the court.

Developmental Influences

Some have suggested that critical periods might exist in the course of a player's development when training interventions would be more or less effective and would fix future training outcomes. The scientific evidence that might support this concept, however, is meager. An adequate investigation into this question would require applying an identical training regimen to the same individuals at different times in their lives (adjusted for body size). This poses methodological issues. It is of interest, though, to examine what is known about certain training responses in immature (prepubertal; less than 12 years of age) players compared with those in mature (postpubertal) players.

When a previously sedentary young adult is placed in a traditional endurance-training program (i.e., running and cycling), $\dot{V}O_2$max is expected to increase by about 15 to 20 percent due to the aerobic training effect. In prepubertal children, however, such a response is blunted, and some studies have indicated no change in $\dot{V}O_2$max over a short-term (12 week) training period. The overall average increase in $\dot{V}O_2$max in this group is only about 5 to 6 percent. It remains unknown just why children have a limited aerobic-training response and what the implications of this finding are for actual endurance performance or extended tennis play.

Researchers once felt that children could not improve muscular strength with resistance training due to lack of circulating androgens. That idea has been thoroughly dispelled. Multiple studies have indicated that the relative magnitude of strength gains with training in both prepubertal boys and girls are equivalent to those observed in adults and that resistance-training programs can be safely conducted in this age group. Indeed, strength training is advocated for children involved in sport for performance gains as well as injury prevention.

That prepubertal children do not thermoregulate as well as adults and are more prone to hyperthermia and heat injury is another myth regarding children in sport that has been dismissed. The original idea was based on the valid observation that children do not sweat as much as adults during exercise (at least in males). However, core temperature increases at the same rate during exercise in the heat in children and adults, levels of dehydration are similar, and episodes of heat injury (i.e., heat exhaustion, heat stroke) are less commonly observed in child athletes than in older competitors.

The idea that there are key windows of opportunity for optimizing a tennis training effect—be it fitness, visuomotor, psychological, or neurological—remains unverified. Many factors contribute to such an effect, and each may be maximized at different ages. For instance, plasticity of neuromuscular influences might occur early in childhood, whereas those factors which augment muscle strength and coordination are important have to wait until puberty. The same might be said regarding hormonal influences on cardiovascular functional responses to training. Mental capacity that permits game sense, strategizing, and commitment to practice are expected to come later with experience.

CHAPTER 9

Visualization Techniques

At this point we can stop to take stock on just what are the aspects of playing tennis over which the player has, quite distinctly, no control and those which he can influence. On one side of the ledger there are those items which he can't change:

- Skill of the opponent
- Rules of the game
- Gravitational laws of physics
- The weather
- Visuomotor coordination (the unconscious automatic player)
- Genetic determinants of talent
- Personality traits

Out on the court, there's really nothing you can do about these things. Yet on the other side of the ledger there is another list (albeit a bit shorter) of those aspects of the game which you can, in fact, control:

- On-court strategy
- Training regimens
- Physical fitness
- Nutrition and hydration
- Mental attitude

Over on the right side are those parts of the game that every player who strives to improve her game targets—the aspects that can be modified, the approaches that offer a chance to gain an advantage over the opponent. Most of these have been previously addressed in these pages. Psychological aspects are an issue which will be addressed in the chapter that follows this one.

In this chapter we'll examine a fascinating new idea that perhaps can be added to the "controlled" side of the ledger— that just by *watching* other players one can acquire tennis skills. It sounds crazy, but there is a neurophysiological basis for believing this, and a limited amount of experimental data exists to back it up as well. Here's the story.

On a hot summer day in Parma, Italy, in 1991, a remarkable event occurred in the research laboratory of Giacomo Rizzolatti and colleagues. The researchers were interested in how nerve cells in the brain of macaque monkeys became electrically activated when these neurons directed motor acts—in this case, monkeys raising their arms to bringing food to their mouths. To this end, the researchers implanted electrodes into the prefrontal cerebral cortex (an area recognized for initiating such actions) of the animals. It was an experimental opportunity to examine brain function.

The story goes that between such trials one of the scientists did what any reasonable person would do: He went out for an ice cream cone. When he returned to the lab, a monkey awaiting its turn in the experiment sat watching him. As the investigator lifted his arm to lick his gelato, the cells in the monkey's brain that are responsible for just that act began to electrically fire.

How could these brain cells, normally responsible for triggering the motor act of bringing food to the animal's own mouth, be activated simply by watching such an action? Rizzolatti recalled that in the past he had seen similar firing of motor brain cells when his monkeys were just watching a human or another animal eating peanuts.[13,14]

Here was a fascinating finding: When an animal visually observed someone else performing an activity, the brain cells responsible for initiating that particular muscular action began to be activated. Rizzolatti and his group, who named these cells mirror neurons, launched the explosive development of new ways of conceiving how the brain directs interactions with its environment.

Subsequent studies confirmed these findings, which were quickly extended to humans as well. Using imaging techniques such as functional magnetic resonance imaging (fMRI), researchers have found increased activity in motor areas of the brain when a person views another person performing an act that is similar to those areas that normally become electrically active when he executes that physical action himself.[6,9,10] The areas of the human brain that appear to contain mirror neurons include those recognized in monkeys but also those that extend to other parts of the brain, such as the primary somatosensory cortex and the posterior middle temporal gyrus.

What's more, the studies in humans indicated that, when one observes another perform an action, mirror neurons could trigger not just motor areas—responsible for performing physical actions—but also feelings and emotions, such as pain, anger, and happiness. To many, the identification of the mirror neuron system is nothing short of a true biological revolution. Mirror neurons permit us to imitate or learn actions from watching others perform them, and through the mirror neuron system we can understand the sentiments and actions of others and actually participate in their emotions and goals.

Learning to play tennis and working to improve game performance require continuous repetition of play (i.e., practice), during which the many components of court play are imprinted into the neuromuscular system. It takes hours of hard work. Might it not be better if a player could simply watch good tennis being played over and over and let her mirror neurons do the work as they trigger the motor patterns in her head?

Learning by watching is not a new idea in the sport-training world. Traditional teaching approaches often include video feedback along with analysis and correction as a means of assessing a player's progress.[21] However, this is about observing expert tennis performance as a means of actually training the motor part of the brain to recreate the action.[5]

Although tennis training through observation and imitation could be a possibility, a big gap exists in the evidence supporting the existence and function of mirror neurons and the idea that one could use such a mirror neuron system to improve tennis performance. Mirror neurons have caused quite a stir in neurophysiological circles, but not all are so convinced that mirror neurons exist in humans.[17] Human studies regarding mirror neurons rely on imaging techniques that show an increase in metabolic activity in areas of motor activity.[3,11,19] But while these have indicated imitative responses to visualization, such responses do not always involve the same regions of the brain that become activated in the studies of monkeys.

The bulk of experiments in humans have been limited to recording which areas of the brain are activated when participants watch or listen to a person perform some action. Some studies have used observed tennis play as the trigger. Michael Wright and Robin Jackson at the Centre for Cognition and Neuroimagery at Brunel University in London used fMRI to show that novice tennis players demonstrated activation of brain areas associated with the mirror neuron network when watching video clips of tennis serve sequences but not when watching video clips of nonaction, such as a bouncing ball.[22]

In another study, participants who knew nothing about playing the guitar watched an instructor play chords and then reproduced the chords. fMRI showed that the same part of the brain lit up when the participants were watching the instructor and when they reproduced the chords. Although this research is far from proving that repeated observation would improve an imitated physical action, such as playing classical guitar or serving in tennis, it provides a biological explanation for how this improvement might actually occur. Tennis players might keep in mind a few observations from studies that have been conducted to date:

- Motor areas in the brain are most strongly excited when someone views a real person performing the action. Watching Wimbledon on television may not be as effective for improving a person's game as viewing the action in person.

- Mirror neurons activate areas in the brain for physical actions that a person has previously experienced. If a person has never served a tennis ball, not much will happen when he observes another individual serving.
- Mirror neuron function is optimized when an object (e.g., a tennis ball) is involved in the observed action.
- The German neuroscientist Violetta Nedelko at the Kliniken Schmieder Allensbach and her colleagues showed that age did not diminish fMRI response of the mirror neuron system in the ventrolateral premotor cortex and inferior parietal cortex to observed or imagined acts.[12]
- Not everyone has the same number of mirror neurons. This raises the question of whether or not one can successfully utilize visualization techniques to improve motor performance.

Observational studies also suggest that mirror neurons have a role in skill development, although the studies are limited.[16,18,23] In 1998, Francisco Atienza and colleagues at Valencia University in Spain examined whether mental training using video demonstrations could enhance tennis serving skills in 9- to 12-year-old intermediate-level female players.[2] Over a 24-week period, four players received only traditional physical training (consisting of techniques, tactics, and fitness) and the other four watched a five-minute video each week in which highly talented players demonstrated ideal serving skills in addition to receiving traditional training. Expert judges evaluated each girl's serve before and after the study period. The players in the physical-practice group showed no significant improvement in service placement or speed, but their scores in technique increased from an average of 4.4 points to 4.6 points. The players in the group that watched video clips improved from 59 to 70 points in the service-speed category and from 4.2 to 5.3 points in technique. The researchers concluded that using videos for visual imitation enhanced tennis service skill in this study. However, because the pool of participants was so small and the measures of improvement were difficult to quantify, these results need to be verified by a larger and

While not conclusive, visual imitation of professional tennis players like German star Sabine Lisicki, shown hitting a forehand during her second round match of the 2013 U.S. Open, can be a useful tool for improving technique in conjunction with loads of physical practice.

David Lobel/Icon SMI

more controlled study before any definite conclusions can be drawn.

I'm going to go out on a limb and suggest that visual imitation is a useful adjunct to lots of physical practice on the tennis court and that the mirror neuron imaging system, or something closely akin to it, is the responsible mechanism. The evidence for this theory is far from conclusive but is certainly promising.

Mental Imaging

Why waste money on Wimbledon tickets when you can imagine a perfect serve? We humans are capable of manufacturing moving pictures in our brains, so why not let motor neurons observe the mind's own visual images to improve your service technique?

Mental imaging is the technique of repeatedly projecting in one's imagination the act of tennis play. Mental imaging has been around for a long time—not just in sport but also in such diverse realms as education, medicine, and music—and many people are convinced that it works. Hundreds of research studies have been performed in an attempt to verify this conclusion (but, unfortunately, most of these studies are considered to be of low scientific quality). There even exists an electronic journal—*Journal of Imagery Research in Sport and Physical Activity*—that is devoted to the subject. Sport psychologist Robert Weinberg at Miami University wrote an article titled "Does Imagery Work?" After reviewing all studies examining the efficacy of mental imagery, he concluded that "the weight of all this evidence most certainly would point to the fact that imagery can positively influence performance."[20]

In mental-imaging studies, participants are typically randomly assigned to one of three experimental conditions: imagery with a positive outcome (e.g., a service ace), imagery with a negative outcome (e.g., a double fault), and control (nonimaging). Most investigations of this type indicate that mental rehearsal of a positive outcome improves performance, whereas negative imaging leads to deterioration. Just how or why mental imaging works remains a mystery. It's possibly all a matter of stimulating motivation. However, fMRI does reveal that objective changes in particular brain centers can be observed when an individual performs mental imaging. This suggests that any positive effects of mental imaging are more than psychological. Evidence also suggests that, in addition to directly improving performance, mental imaging might enhance mental skills that influence performance. For example, it might increase self-confidence, suppress competitive anxiety, and improve motivation.

However, because this body of research certainly has its limitations, the final answer regarding the efficacy of mental imaging isn't in. Some studies have assessed the effects of mental imaging when used just before an athletic competition rather than as a training tool. In such studies, the specific effectiveness of mental imaging is often difficult to isolate because it was used along with other mental skills, such as relaxation. It is difficult to verify whether the research participants actually used valid imaging techniques, and very few studies have been conducted in real competitive situations.

Also, not all research information on mental imaging in tennis is consistent. For example, Ricardo Weigert Coelho and colleagues at the Research Center for Exercise and Sport Science at the Federal University of Paraná in Brazil demonstrated that a combination of observation and mental imagery improved serve accuracy in national-level 16- to 18-year-old tennis players but that this intervention had no effect on skill in the serve return.[4] The authors felt that this finding was consistent with the idea that the athlete can precisely visualize the serve in his mind because it is a predictable motion that the server controls. The serve return, on the other hand, is unpredictable and thus cannot be so easily imagined visually.

However, Nicolas Robin and colleagues in the Laboratoire Performance, Motricite et Cognition in Poitiers, France, showed that 15 sessions of imagery training improved the accuracy of serve returns in experienced French players.[14] This study also examined the extent to which a player has the ability to create mental images. They found that good imagers (as determined by a questionnaire) had better results than poor imagers, although the latter still showed more improvement than nonimaging participants.

The general consensus is that these investigations support the idea that repeated mental imaging of a motor task or complex sport skill can improve performance of that task or skill, at least to some extent. However, these studies suggest that mental imaging is not as effective as physical training, so one still has to put in the hours of organized practice. But, for many people, mental imaging appears to help.

The following tips and guidelines might help optimize your ability to gain skill via mental visualization training.

- Create an image of tennis play as viewed from the stands or put yourself right into the action on the court. While you yourself might be the player you are portraying in this brain video, it is probably best to use your favorite professional tennis player, who is likely a superior model.
- Don't just close your eyes and watch your mind's imagery —get right in there and make it real. Sense the kinesthetic motion of your muscles as they move. Feel the heat and sweat. Hear the crowd roar and the racket striking the ball.
- Perform mental imaging in a peaceful environment for at least 15 minutes 2 or 3 times a week.
- Studies indicate that mental imagining can be effective in youths as well as the elderly.
- Watch it as the action occurs. Researchers initially believed that imagining in slow motion was better because it allowed more time to focus on different parts of the physical act. Now, however, most sport psychologists feel that you should imagine in real time because you want your brain to learn the motion as you're going to use it— at full speed.
- Try it with some soothing Debussy or Tchaikovsky. At least one study suggests that background music may make mental imaging more successful.

Imagery in Training

Using imagery in tennis training has some scientific merit now that evidence of a neurophysiological basis exists. While we await further validation, it is reasonable to conclude that visual imagery, in the form of either imagination or observation, can improve tennis performance in some individuals. Are there particular advantages of using such techniques as opposed to, say, putting in a few more hours with the ball machine? Let's explore this question using the model for learning tennis described in chapter 3.

When a physical act is performed repeatedly over time, as in sport training, the neuromuscular pathways responsible for that action become more effective.[21] As a consequence, the physical performance outcome—be it speed, strength, coordination, or a complex task, such as a tennis serve—improves. Errors are reduced and variability in execution of the task decreases. In this process, motor memory is created. The neurophysiological changes that affect this improvement remain largely unknown, but newer brain imaging techniques have identified regions of the brain that are responsible.

Researchers believe that acquisition of sport skills through physical training occurs in stages that represent points on a continuum of how much conscious thought one puts into performing the skill (see chapter 3). Skill performance starts with conscious effort and moves to subconscious action that one executes without thinking. The thinking player always gives way to the automatic player.

Choking Under Pressure

You have match point in the finals of the city tournament. You've climbed back from a set down and the crowd is behind you. Despite your achievement of sport expertise, your body suddenly betrays you and you double fault, the second serve sailing beyond the service line. You've just choked. Your opponent takes the next two points and the trophy. Under the pressure of performing in the moment, what normally would be easy and rote turns into a disaster. Considering the universality of such experiences and their devastating effect on athletes, sport psychologists and now neurophysiologists have given considerable thought to this problem. Here's the commonly accepted explanation of "choking" in the framework of the traditional model of sport skill acquisition.

In the process of learning a sport, a player advances from an initial stage of a conscious, directed focus on the individual elements of a tennis serve (e.g., ball toss, aiming the serve, grip, action on the ball, leaning forward) to a stage of automaticity in which the brain permits the player to serve without thinking about all the factors that go into it. The player could at this point serve perfectly well even while considering what to have for dinner.

In pressure situations when a lot is on the line, the player worries and the conscious self comes back into play and tries to direct the performance. The player, in essence, reverts back to the starting stages of the learning process. All this thinking and worrying blocks and interferes with the automatic tennis skills the player spent so much time honing. The predictable result is a serve that slams into the net.

Training using visual imagery might help reduce the risk of choking in critical competitive situations. It makes sense that the less one uses cognitive methods to learn a sport technique the less the conscious mind might interfere in crucial performance situations. Visual learning, whether through observation of others or mental imaging, facilitates the acquisition of technique into the automatic parts of your mental machinery. This process *bypasses* the conscious mind. When a player watches a perfect serve, the motor centers responsible for that action imitate the many components of the serve without the mind consciously sorting them out. Therefore, one could predict that reversion to conscious interference would be less likely when the pressure's on.

Imagery in Deliberate Practice

As discussed in chapter 4, Anders Ericsson and colleagues at Florida State University believe that no genetic limits on performance capabilities exist and that prolonged intense practice leads to steady improvement in performance and the achievement of elite skill levels.[6] This idea flies in the face of the traditional dogma that to become a champion athlete one must choose his or her parents carefully. Most people would accept the idea that to become a top-level athlete a player must be highly committed to an extended intensive training regimen.

Professor Jennifer Cumming and Craig Hall at the University of Birmingham in the United Kingdom contend that mental imagery, practiced as either a supplement to or sub-stitute for physical training, can play an important role in training programs involving deliberate practice. According to these researchers, the same degree of effort and concentration that Ericsson and colleagues considered critical to performance improvement can be attained through mental imagery as well as through deliberate physical practice. They predict that a linear relationship exists between time spent in deliberate im-agery practice and performance, based on evidence suggesting that high-level athletes use mental imaging more often and more effectively than less-elite athletes do. If true, this would parallel the observations of a similar relationship between hours of deliberate physical practice and performance in musi-cians and athletes.

Visual imaging might prove useful in other ways. The downside of engaging in deliberate physical practice is the risk of incurring injury, burnout, and motivational fatigue—all rec-ognized outcomes of excessive training. Mental imaging and observational training could be a substitute for some of the de-liberate physical practice, thereby reducing the risk of these complications. Mental practice could allow a high level of training with less physical stress. Also, an athlete could use visual training when sidelined by a physical injury in order to permit progress to continue even when she is not on the court.

Imagery and Coaches

One can find a considerable amount of enthusiasm among tennis coaches regarding visual imagery techniques as a means of training players. In the fall of 2012, I had the opportunity to talk with Paul Arciero, an exercise physiologist who has spent 32 years as a talented player and coach at every level, in-cluding a stint as head tennis coach at Skidmore College.

> Throughout this time I've incorporated visual imagery into my coaching as a standard training technique. The response from my players has been very positive, and I still hold that utilizing this technique was the primary reason my teams (which often comprised players with

much less tennis pedigree and experience than other top-ranked teams) were able to compete with the best around. In my opinion, there's no question that we "groove" our nervous system to perform better by both physical and visual training. I know it has helped me when I go through periods when I'm not playing much. So "dreaming" about playing that perfect match comes in handy when I return.[1]

However, not all are so enchanted. Anders Ericsson, not a coach but rather a psychologist who advocates the concept of deliberate practice, states:

> My problem is that I have not so far seen how somebody could improve performance by imaging. In particular, how someone could do something (i.e., attain a reproducible level of performance) that is beyond their current performance by imagery practice. The reason is, where is the feedback coming from when you engage in imagery?[7]

However, considerable enthusiasm exists among coaches and players alike for the benefits of visual training using either the traditional mental-imaging approach or imitation through mirror neurons. These techniques presently lack a sound experimental foundation, but investigative techniques such as fMRI are beginning to verify what players and coaches have long thought: Visual imagery as a means of improving tennis play has a biological basis that is part of the plasticity of human performance with training.

CHAPTER 10

Match Mind-Set

There is a sign in a souvenir shop in Carcassonne, France, that reads "Le muscle le plus important au tennis c'est le cerveau," which translates as "The most important muscle in tennis is the brain." Everyone from the casual fan to the seasoned veteran knows that mental aspects of tennis have a big role in determining one's success on the court. A player can perfect a nasty backhand slice, purchase a high-tech racket, and take hours of costly lessons, but if his head isn't in the right place or if he doesn't possess the right mental skills, he's not going to fare well. The psychological aspects of tennis are a critical part of the game.

Tennis experts have tried to estimate how much mental attributes dominate the game. I suggest that it depends on the level of the player's skill: The higher a player's ranking, the greater the relative mental contribution. In the semifinals at Roland Garros, all of the players have roughly the same technical skills and level of fitness. The mental part of the game plays the predominant role in deciding the winner. At the other end of the scale, a beginner's major objective is learning enough technical skill just to keep the ball in the court. Mental abilities come later.

Mental Skills

We first need to define the term *mental fitness* to know what psychological attributes are relevant to tennis success. Sport psychologist Dan Gould and colleagues at Michigan State University surveyed a large group of junior tennis coaches on the importance and nature of training the mental skills of young, high-level players.[7] Not surprisingly, all coaches surveyed agreed that mental skills are critical to tennis success. Their opinions are interesting.

- On average, the coaches felt that 80 percent of their players had difficulties with the mental aspects of tennis and that these problems held them back from performing at their full potential.
- The coaches believed that almost 60 percent of the players had parents who interfered with the mental part of their child's tennis game.
- The mental skills considered most important to tennis success were enjoyment and fun, focus and concentration, self-confidence, emotional control, honesty and integrity, motivation and passion, practice intensity, and positive thinking and self-talk.
- The mental skills considered most difficult to teach were emotional control, motivation, self-confidence, and crisis management.

The list of mental skills also includes passion, positive thinking, emotional control, commitment, determination, adaptability, gamesmanship, and what psychologist Maureen Weiss has termed "various forms of hyphenated constructs": self-confidence, self-image, self-concept, and self-esteem. These are the mental qualities and attitudes that help translate fitness and technical skills into winning—and enjoyable—tennis.[4]

Positive mental attitudes do not originate when a player sets foot onto the tennis court. From a psychological perspective, the mental features that contribute to how people play tennis are the same ones that distinguish people as individual beings in the context of the world we live in, including personal relationships, work, and goals. The following paragraphs discuss some of the psychological characteristics that can make or break a player.

Forward Thinking

At the 2012 Wimbledon tournament, as tennis fans were re-covering from the shock of witnessing Rafael Nadal fall to a little-known opponent the day before, Roger Federer was down two sets to zip to 29th-seeded Julien Benneteau. Just as disaster appeared to be ready to strike, the six-time champion turned it around and took the third set 6-2. In the fourth set, at 6-6 in the tie break, Federer was two points from the end. Seemingly undaunted, he took the next two points and then the final set, 6-1. Everyone sat awestruck. How did he do that? At the point when most people would have dissolved in tears, the Great Swiss pulled himself back from the abyss. What was the explanation?

Federer said to a television interviewer after that match, "You just have to try to play tough and focus point for point. Sounds so boring, but it's the right thing to do out there." Champions concentrate on the now and do not dwell on failures in the past. To be at the top of the game, one must have a very limited short-term memory in order to forget those horrendous blunders and just move on.

The next day at Wimbledon, a wild card entry from Ka-zakhstan named Yaroslava Shvedova played a perfect first set in her third-round match against Sara Errani of Italy, winning every single point. It was the only time in 44 years of women's professional competition that a player has won 24 points in a row. Incredibly, Shvedova didn't know it was happening. She told reporters afterwards that she just kept her concentration on each point. Keeping one's mind on the game for each point is what focusing is all about.

Motivation

Motivation involves the will to win and the drive to succeed—both of which are critical—as well as the psychological capacity to persist over many years of intense tennis training. Predicting future athletic success based on physical performance and an-thropometric features has been fraught with failure. The best single markers of future talent seem to be the psychological

As Roger Federer illustrates in match after match, intense focus is a critical component of successful play.

Robert Deutsch-USA TODAY Sports

factors associated with motivation, including coachability, self-confidence, and goal orientation.[1] As tennis coach and researcher Piotr Unierzyski at the University School of Physical Education in Poznan, Poland, emphasized, "It often causes disappointment that . . . players who do not possess high level of achievement motivation do not reach the highest levels of the [tennis] game despite good results at a young age."[13]

Confidence

Not long ago it seemed that Novak Djokovic had met a road-block. Rising rapidly in the professional tennis ranks, he arrived at number three in the world. However, he couldn't find a way to subdue Rafael Nadal and Roger Federer ahead of him.

There he sat, idling at number three. Finally, he took out Federer in five sets at the U.S. Open in 2010, and the dam burst. He went on to notch an unbelievable 43 straight wins along with 10 titles in 2010 (he beat Nadal in six of those), and by midyear he reached his coveted goal: number one men's player in the world. How did he accomplish this—and so suddenly? A list of possibilities was tossed around in the press: his new gluten-free diet, stepped-up training regimen, improved fitness, and spiritual guidance. But what seemed obvious to most was that he now *believed* that he could beat those two guys. Once he knew it, his confidence and performance took a quantum leap.

Goal-Driven Training and Performance

Tennis players know that mental toughness is important. But in the midst of frustrating losses, blown leads, and wayward backhands, the means of achieving such psychological strengths often seems elusive. Players want to know how to gain mental strength on the court, if these attributes can be learned or if we are constrained by our own individual personalities, and if these features are heritable or if they are all driven by our subconscious mind?

Psychologists have developed some helpful models that can be used to categorize tennis behavior.[12] According to goal perspective theory, a player's approach to the game can be identified as either task involved or ego involved. A task-involved player is focused on learning and playing the game as a means toward self-improvement, whereas an ego-involved player focuses on outplaying others. The criterion of success for the task-oriented player is working hard to advance skill, whereas that of the ego-oriented player is victory over the opponent. A player who is task involved recognizes that certain extrinsic factors (e.g., weather, opponent skill) can't be changed and are out of one's control, whereas a player who is ego involved believes that these factors define her success on the court.

Task orientation is the healthier route. Research indicates that ego-oriented players exhibit greater anxiety and impaired concentration on the court. These individuals tend to be unhappy and dissatisfied and more often suffer burnout from the sport. Task orientation, on the other hand, leads to a stronger work ethic, higher levels of success, and greater personal satisfaction with the game.

Those who have their goal perspectives straight—who focus on doing their best and forget about the competition—end up happier and better players. Research shows that such attitudes can be best fostered through significant others. One should select coaches and peers who support player improvement rather than those who value a player based on his ranking or win–loss record. Relationships with supportive individuals are critical in establishing a positive environment that promotes self-esteem and a proper perspective on success and failure on the court.

In the goal perspective theory, the motivational climate of tennis changes as one moves up the ladder of success and level of competition. A player can't be Rafael Nadal without a bit of ego orientation. Researchers Miguel Crespo at the International Tennis Federation in Valencia, Spain, and Australian Machar Reid pointed out:

> General indications are that tennis becomes more ego involved as players move from beginner to competitive tennis. That is, at the beginner level, task-oriented motivational climates are important in enhancing player motivation and enjoyment. At advanced levels, an ego-involving motivational climate might precipitate, yet coaches should be task-involving in their interactions with players during training and before and after competition.[3]

Other models have been suggested for describing and explaining psychological aspects such as motivation in tennis. Competence motivation theory holds that motivation in tennis play reflects a desire to be perceived (by both one's self and others) as a competent individual. This idea has been expanded into a socially oriented theory that sees the player seeking to win as a need for gaining the approval of others.

Learning Mental Skills

A competitive tennis player needs to step onto the court with the right mental attitude. Some issues here are key. The extent that mental toughness—developing the psychological traits important for tennis success—can be learned is controversial. But most would agree that for the serious competitor mental training is just as necessary as technical and physical-fitness training.

For eons, psychologists have been interested in the extent to which personality traits are inherited or a result of environmental influences. At present, the general consensus seems to be that certain behavioral traits are a product of one's genes, whereas others are a product of sociocultural influences.

It may be that certain mental traits can be learned, whereas others are already immutable by the time one gets on the court. It may be that the mental qualities seen in high-level players are characteristics that have enabled them to become star athletes. But conversely, perhaps tennis training, which involves learning positive psychological skills, makes these players what they are.

Dr. Martin Seligman, an eminent psychologist at the University of Pennsylvania, has devoted his career to documenting the self-destructive effects of pessimistic thinking and demonstrating techniques that one can learn to replace negative attitudes with optimistic, positive attitudes.[11] Seligman supports a cure by cognitive therapy, which holds that it is possible for individuals to control what they think and that by altering the thought process one can substitute positive for reflexive negative thoughts.

Learned optimism by cognitive therapy consists of two key strategies: distraction and disputation. With distraction, the individual learns how to block out reflexive negative thoughts that pop up when she makes an error by focusing on something else, such as the next point, a song, or a couple deep breaths. With disputation, the individual consciously changes how she mentally reacts to an error by considering a more positive and usually realistic response. For example, a player misses a shot because she took her eye off the ball. The pessimistic response: "I never watch the ball!!" The optimistic response: "He hit a nifty slice, so I lost sight of the ball. I'll be ready for that next time."

Seligman's approach has served as the basis for many of the recommendations that sport psychologists use in counseling their athletes. A tennis player can find at the local bookstore a plethora of advice on how to step on the court and face opponents with the proper mind-set. There doesn't seem to be anything particularly magical about this advice. Sports psychologists often advocate Seligman's idea that optimism is a powerful weapon and an effective means of optimizing (and enjoying) one's game. When a player makes an error, he should accept it as part of the game and get it out of his head as quickly as possible. This takes effort and mental training, and it comes easier for some than for others. But practicing mental toughness—blocking out reflexive negative thoughts—works.

Tennis coaches don't need to be persuaded that the mental attitudes of their players can be enhanced. When Aidan Moran, a psychologist at University College in Dublin, surveyed 30 full-time tennis coaches, all of the coaches but one indicated that they thought psychological skills can be improved with training and practice.[9] The techniques they considered most useful were (in order of effectiveness)

1. positive self-talk,
2. imagery of the next shot,
3. imagery of tactics,
4. setting performance goals,
5. taking deep breaths,
6. slowing down behavior,
7. preshot routines, and
8. trigger words.

But maybe these behaviors simply fit into the category of preshot routines, along with such illustrious examples as elite players who readjust their shirts and turn their backs to their opponent between points, tugging at their racket strings

Moran notes that major gaps in knowledge about the psychology of tennis remain. For example, it's unclear what players themselves think of these methods of acquiring mental skills, what specific effects these methods have on player performance, and whether players have problems remembering when to use these methods in the heat of a match.

Choking

Finals of the Australian Open, fifth set tie break, score is 8-9, the first serve is long. Sports fans live for moments such as these that provide the drama that makes sport so enjoyable. Certainly some athletes thrive on the adrenaline-filled moments that provide their greatest challenges. The rest of us seek the excitement we get when we compete, but this level of tension may be a bit more than we bargained for.

In the stress of the moment a player may fear she'll fold—double-fault with a second serve that barely reaches the bottom of the net. She chokes. It's not the do-or-die situation itself that makes her fail but rather the anxiety—the gnawing dread of failure—that mounts at the time. How does one deal with such moments?

Dealing with competitive stress, particularly when it all comes to a head in win-or-lose moments, is a challenge for all athletes. Performance failure in these situations occurs when the thinking player (the one in a player's conscious thoughts) interferes with the actions of the automatic player (the one that conducts actions without a player's conscious thought). With years of practice and experience the automatic player develops an effective serve, but as soon as the thinking player begins to try to control what's going on, the automatic player gets befuddled. That's just what one does when everything is on the line in crucial competitive situations. The most disastrous thing a player can do in this situation is try his best to perform the serve or shot because the thinking player takes control. He has to have faith in the automatic player. However, that's easier said than done when one is concentrating on not concentrating. Therefore, the traditional strategies for preventing a meltdown in crisis situations come down to figuring out how to not think.

A number of authors have offered means for not thinking when it's all on the line. Foremost on the list of required reading for all young players is Timothy Gallwey's *The Inner Game of Tennis,* which players should at least skim before every big match.[5] Gallwey provides the basic strategy for avoiding this "over-thinking": "Quieting the mind means less thinking, calculating, judging, worrying, fearing, hoping, trying, re-gretting, controlling, jittering, or distracting . . . . The question naturally arises: 'How can I still the mind?' Or 'How can I keep from thinking on the tennis court?' The answer is simple: Just stop!"

Another good read is *Choke,* in which author Sian Beilock concludes that "paralysis by analysis" is caused by the "dangers of thinking too much."[2] That's when our bodies let us down in those high pressure situations just when, paradoxically, we need to performing at our best.[2] Following are some ideas from these sources on how keep it steady when the going gets tough.

- **Preparation.** If you're going to turn things over to your automatic player in times of maximum stress, your per-formance needs to be down pat. You can't have confi-dence in your automatic player if you haven't gained con-fidence in its ability. So practice, get it right, and get com-fortable with your abilities.
- **Rehearsal.** Research has provided a concrete means for diminishing or avoiding performance failure in tight situa-tions: Rehearse them. Create stress and anxiety during practice workouts to get used to it. If you've never been at match point in a third set tie break, your odds of keeping cool are low when the real thing comes around. However, if you've confronted anxiety during practice, the outlook is better. You can rehearse mentally by visualizing high-pressure situations or by recruiting some meaningful others—coaches, parents, fellow players, the person who will be making the decision on your college tennis schol-arship—to watch you perform. You can bet with

somebody on your serve success. All of these help you rehearse for the real thing in competition.

In a study by Raoul Oudejans and Rob Pijpers of the faculty of human movement sciences at Vrije University in Amsterdam, 17 expert basketball players shot free throws with and without induced anxiety over a five-week period.[10] Stress was created by filming the players and telling them that experts would review the footage, offering financial rewards to the teams that did best, and asking the players to visualize a game situation in which the free throw would be decisive for victory. Compared with a control (nonstress) group, the stress group showed greater success in an anxiety situation on the posttest.

- **Focus.** The challenges are how to prevent the thinking player from trying to undo the efforts of the talented automatic player and how to prevent the fear of failure. One answer: Focus your conscious mind so onto something else so strongly that there's no way negative thoughts can creep in. It's not easy. When you try hard not to think, the usual result is the opposite—you think more. Again, you have to practice. Don't wait until a critical time of competitive stress to focus.

  Take a deep breath. Talk to yourself in a positive manner. Repeat a one-word mantra. Concentrate on where the serve is going to land. Hum your favorite song. Pretend you are Andre Agassi. Empty your mind, like deleting computer files. Or make up your own focus.

- **Don't tarry.** The usual advice for dealing with competitive anxiety, particularly if you're falling behind in a match, is to slow things down. Avoid the tendency to rush. Take a few moments before serving. Maybe giving your opponent some time to think about his current success might break his rhythm. However, some sport psychologists have advised doing the opposite in those critical, do-or-die moments of competition. Sitting and contemplating the importance of the moment might give your thinking player time to destroy your automatic player. Move ahead and hit the serve.

This ability to perform in high-pressure situations is what separates the elite from the non-elite tennis player. On the biggest stages, in the most gut-wrenching points, elite players stay focused and concentrate. What's their secret? The answer does not seem available to the common man. Author David Foster Wallace, himself a top junior player, lamented this in an essay in *Consider the Lobster*.

> It is not an accident that great athletes are often called "naturals" because they can, in performance, be totally present: they can proceed on instinct and muscle-memory and autonomic will such that agent and action are one. The real secret behind top athletes' genius, then, may be as esoteric and obvious and dull and profound as silence itself. The real, many-veiled answer to the question of just what goes through a great player's mind as he stands at the center of hostile crowd-noise and lines up the free-throw that will decide the game might well be: *nothing at all*.[14]

Hans Ulrich Gumbrecht of Stanford agrees: "Athletes' performance may indeed improve in proportion to the distance they gain from consciousness and from the realm of intentions."[8]

Thinking and Not Thinking

Playing tennis is an extraordinarily complex motor act that relies on accurate visual tracking, a finely tuned timing mechanism, and a coordinated cascade of muscle innervation and contraction. And that's just to strike the ball. A whole set of mental attitudes are critical to tennis success, not just in performance but in commitment to the long time it takes to mold an expert player. Players need to think to strategize on the court, stay hydrated, and regulate the tempo of play.

Many of these functions are conducted below the level of consciousness, whereas others depend on careful thinking. We have seen that one of these mental processes may interfere with another, such as when thinking about striking an effective serve at a critical moment may actually have the opposite effect. But the skillful player needs to think, too.

The knowledgeable player needs to know when to think and when to have faith and keep the conscious mind in check. Table 10.1 offers guidelines that may be laminated and consulted during set changeovers.

As tennis player, coach, and television commentator Brad Gilbert and Steve Jamison point out in *Winning Ugly*, players need to know what's happening in the match.[6] How is it going? Who's doing what to whom? What's working for the opponent? Is she taking control of the net, or is her smashing forehand flying past you down the line? Are you making too many unforced errors, trying too many high-risk shots, or playing too passively? Only in thoughtfully analyzing the answers to these questions can a player strategize about what to emphasize, what to change, or what new plan to use. Gilbert and Jamison contend that many of us need to do more of this.

> Most recreational tennis players don't know who's doing what to whom during their match. They don't pay attention. They don't observe and analyze what's going on . . . . You need to understand what's going on in the match, with your game, your opponent's game, and with the interaction of the two.[6]

TABLE 10.1   Thinking on the Tennis Court

Think	Do not think
About how you are losing points	About the last egregious error
About drinking at each set changeover	About the score
About watching the ball intently	About plans for dinner
About maintaining confident body language	About your place on the club tennis ladder
Positive thoughts	Negative thoughts
"I love playing tennis"	"I hate playing tennis"

BIBLIOGRAPHY

Preface

1. Wallace, D.F. 1196. Infinite jest. New York:Back Bay Books.

Chapter 1

1. Barret, J. 2001. *Wimbledon: The official history of the championships*. London: Collins Willow.
2. Bartlett, M., and B. Gillen, eds. 1981. *The tennis book*. New York: Arbor House.
3. Gleick, J. 1999. *Faster: The acceleration of just about everything*. New York: Vintage Books.
4. Gonzales, P. 1964. The serve and how to vary it. In *How to play tennis the professional way*, ed. A. Trengrove,. New York: Simon & Schuster.
5. Hurtado, P. 1984. Racqueteering: Or how tennis learned to string tightly and carry a big stick. *Tennis West* April: 12-15.
6. Kramer, J. 1948. *Playing tennis my way*. New York: Ziff Davis.
7. Schickel, R. 1975. *Forest Hills: The twelve-day week*. New York: Ridge Press.
8. Sumner, A. 2011. *Court on canvas: Tennis in art*. London: Philip Wilson.
9. Wallace, D.F. 2012. *Both flesh and not*. New York: Little, Brown.

Chapter 2

1. Bakewell, S. 2010. *How to live: Or, a life of Montaigne*. New York: Other Press, p. 112.
2. Brody, H. 2006. Unforced errors and error reduction in tennis. *Br J Sports Med* 40:397-400.
3. Crespo, M, and M.M. Reid. 2007. Motivation in tennis. *Br J Sports Med* 41:769-772.
4. Deaner, H, and J.M. Silva. 2002. Personality and sport performance. In *Psychological foundation of sport*, ed. J.M. Silva and D.C. Stevens, 48-65. Boston: Allyn & Bacon.
5. Halinan, J.T. 2009. *Why we make mistakes*. New York: Broadway Books.
6. Ivanitsky, A.M., I.V. Kurnitskaya, and S. Sobotka. 1986. Cortical topography of event-related potentials to winning and losing a video tennis game. *Int J Psychophysiol* 4:149-155.
7. Lehrer, J. 2009. *How we decide*. Boston: Mariner Books.

Chapter 3

1. Bengtsson, S.L., Z. Nagy, S. Skare, L. Forsman, H. Forssberg, F. Ullen F. 2005. Extensive piano practicing has regionally specific effects on white matter development. *Nat Neurosci* 8: 1148-1150.
2. Bezzola, L., S. Merillat, C. Gaser, and L. Jancke. 2011. Training-induced neural plasticity in golf novices. *J Neurosci* 31:12444-12448.
3. Bryan, W.L., and N. Harter. 1899. Studies on the telegraphic language: The acquisition of a hierarchy of habits. *Psychol Rev* 6: 345-375.
4. Coyle D. 2009. The talent code. New York: Bantam Books.
5. Draganski, B., C. Gaser, G. Kempermann, H.G. Kuhn, J. Winkle, C. Buchel, A. May. 2006. Temporal and spatial dynamics of brain structure changes during extensive learning. J Neurosc 26: 6314-6317.
6. Fields, R.D. 2011. Imaging learning: The search for a memory trace. *Neuroscience* 17:185-196.
7. Floyer-Lea, A., and P.M. Matthews. 2004. Changing brain networks for visuomotor control with increased movement automaticity. *J Neurophysiol* 92: 2405-2412.
8. Halsband, U., and R.K. Lange. 2006. Motor learning in man: A review of functional and clinical studies. *J Physiol* 99: 414-424.
9. Hanggi, J., S. Koeneke L. Bezzola, L. Jancke. 2010. Structural neuroplasticity in the sensorimotor network of professional female ballet dancers. *Hum Brain Mapp* 31: 1196-1206.
10. Hebb, D.O. 1949. *The organization of behavior*. New York: Wiley.
11. Imfield, A., M.S. Oechslin, M. Meyer, T. Loenneker, L. Jancke. 2009. White matter plasticity in the corticospinal tract of musicians: a diffusion tensor imaging study. *Neuroimage* 46: 600-607.
12. Jancke, L. 2009. The plastic human brain. *Res Neurol Neurosci* 27:521-538.
13. Kleim, J.A., E. Lussnig, E.R. Schwarz, T.A. Comery, W.T. Greenough. 1996. Synaptogenesis and FOS expression in the motor cortex of the adult rat after motor skill learning. *J Neurosci* 16: 4529-4535.
14. Knaepen, K., M. Goekint, E.M. Heyman, and R. Meeusen. 2010. Neuroplasticity-exercise-induced response of peripheral brain-derived neurotrophic factor: A systematic review of experimental studies in human subjects. *Sports Med* 40: 765-801.
15. Lehrer, J. 2007. *Proust was a neuroscientist*. Boston: Houghton Mifflin.
16. Pearce, A.J., G.W. Thickbroom, M.L.Byrnes, F.L. Mastaglia. 2000 Functional reorganization of the corticomotor projection to the hand of skilled racquet players. *Exp Brain Res* 130: 238-243.
17. Reid, M., M. Crespo, B. Lay, and J. Berry. 2007. Skill acquisition in tennis: Research and current practice. *J Science Med Sport* 10: 1-10.
18. Sanes J.R., J.W. Lichtman. 1999. Can molecules explain long-term potentiation? *Nat Neurosci* 2: 597-604.
19. Summers, J.J. 2005. A historical perspective on skill acquisition. In *Skill acquisition in sport: Research, theory, and practice*, ed. A.M. William and N.J. Hodges, 1-26. New York: Routledge.

20. Tyc, F., and A. Boyadjian. 2006. Cortical plasticity and motor activity studied with transcranial magnetic stimulation. *Rev Neurosci* 17: 469-495.
21. Ungerleider, L.G., J. Doyon, and A. Karni. 2002. Imaging brain plasticity during motor skill learning. *Neurobiol Learn Mem* 78: 553-564.
22. van Praag, H. 2009. Exercise and the brain: Something to chew on. *Trends Neurosci* 32: 283-290.
23. Zoladz, J.A., and A. Pilc. 2010. The effect of physical activity on the brain de-rived neurotrophic factor: From animal to human studies. *J Physiol Pharmacol* 61: 533-541.

Chapter 4

1. Bouchard, C., R.M. Malina, and L. Perusse. 1997. *Genetics of fitness and physical performance*. Champaign, IL: Human Kinetics.
2. Ericsson, K.A., R.T. Krampe, and C. Tesch-Romer. 1993. The role of deliberate practice in the acquisition of expert performance. *Psych Rev* 100: 363-406.
3. Ericsson, K.A., K. Nandagopal, and R.W. Roring. 2009. Toward a science of exceptional achievement: Attaining superior performance through deliberate practice. *Ann NY Acad Sci* 1172:199-217.
4. Goldspink, G., and C.P. Velloso. 2008. Genetics and human performance: Natural selection and genetic modification. In *Physiological bases of human per-formance during work and exercise*, ed. N.A.S. Taylor and H. Groeller, 135-148. Edinburgh: Churchill Livingstone.
5. Heathcote, A., S. Brown, and D.J.K. Mewhort. 2000. The power law repeated: The case for an exponential law of practice. *Psych Bull Rev* 7:185-207.
6. Lucia, A., M. Moran, H. Zihong, and J.R. Ruiz. 2010. Elite athletes: Are the genes the champions? *Int J Sports Physiol Perf* 5: 98-102.
7. Puthucheary, Z., J.R.A. Skipworth, J. Rawal, M. Loosemore, K. Van Someren, and H.E. Montgomery. 2011. Genetic influences in sport and physical per-formance. *Sports Med* 41: 845-859.
8. Rankinen, T., and C. Bouchard. 2012. Genetic differences in the relationships among physical activity, fitness, and health. In *Physical activity and health* (2nd ed.), ed. C. Bouchard, S.N. Blair, and W.L. Haskell, 381-408. Cham-paign, IL: Human Kinetics.
9. Stratton, S.M., Y.-T. Liu, S. Hong, G. Mayer-Kress, and K.M. Newell. 2007. Snoddy (1926) revisited: Time scales of motor learning. *J Motor Behav* 39: 503-515.
10. Tucker, R., and M. Collins. 2012. What makes champions? A review of the relative contribution of genes and training to sporting success. *Br J Sports Med* 46: 555-561.

Chapter 5

1. Abbott, A., and D. Collins. 2004. Eliminating the dichotomy between theory and practice in talent identification and development: Considering the role of psychology. *J Sports Sci* 22: 395-408.
2. Agassi, A. 2009. *Open: An autobiography*. New York: Knopf.

3. Baker, J. 2003. Early specialization in youth sport: A requirement for adult expertise? *High Abil Stud* 14: 85-94.
4. Bompa, T.O. 2000. *Total training for young champions*. Champaign, IL: Human Kinetics.
5. Bompa, T.O. Conversation with author.
6. Coté, J. 1999. The influence of the family in the development of talent in sports. *Sports Psychol*. 13: 395-417.
7. Coté, J., J. Baker, and B. Abernethy. 2003. From play to practice: A developmental framework for the acquisition of expertise in team sports. In *Expert performance in sports: Advances in research on sports expertise*, ed. J.L. Starkes and K.A. Ericsson, 89-114. Champaign, IL: Human Kinetics.
8. Coyle, D. 2007. How to grow a super-athlete. *New York Times*, March 4.
9. Dwyre, B. 2010. USTA message of player development is overdone and unnecessary. *Los Angeles Times*, September 6.
10. Ericsson, K.A., K. Nandagopal, and R.W. Roring. 2009. Toward a science of exceptional achievement: Attaining superior performance through deliberate practice. *Ann NY Acad Sci* 1172: 199-217.
11. Helsen, W.F., N.J. Hodges, J. Van Winckel, and J.L. Starkes. 2000. The roles of talent, physical precocity and practice in the development of soccer expertise. *J Sport Sci* 18:727-736.
12. Malina, R.M. 2009. Children and adolescents in the sport culture: The overwhelming majority to the select few. *J Exerc Sci Fit* 7(Suppl.): S1-S10.
13. Malina, R.M. 2010. Early sport specialization: Roots, effectiveness, risks. *Curr Sports Med Rep* 9: 364-371.
14. McEnroe, J. 2002. *You cannot be serious*. New York: Putnam's Sons.
15. Monsaas, J.A. 1985. Learning to be a world-class tennis player. In *Developing talent in young people*, ed. B.S. Bloom, 211-269. New York: Ballantine.
16. Rowland, T.W. 2011. *The athlete's clock*. Champaign, IL: Human Kinetics.
17. Vaeyens, R., M. Lenoir, A.M. Williams, and R.M. Philippaerts. 2008. Talent identification and development programmes in sport. *Sports Med* 38: 703-714.

Chapter 6

1. Brody, H. 2006. Unforced errors and error reduction in tennis. *Br J Sports Med* 40: 397-404.
2. Brody, H., R. Cross, and C. Lindsey. 2002. *The physics and technology of tennis*. Visa, CA: Racquet Tech.
3. Cole, K.C. 1999. *First you build a cloud: And other reflections on physics as a way of life*. New York: Mariner Books.
4. Cropper, W.H. 2001. *Great physicists*. Oxford: Oxford University Press.
5. Groppel, J. 1992. *High tech tennis*. Champaign, IL: Human Kinetics.
6. Hamill, J. 2012. Personal Communication.
7. Mead, T.P., J.N. Drowatsky, and L. Hardin-Crosby. 2000. Positive and negative stimuli in relation to tennis players' reaction time. *Percept Mot Skills* 90: 236-240.

8. Shim, J., L.G. Carlton, and Y-H Kwon. 2006. Perception of kinematic characteristics of tennis strokes for anticipating stroke type and direction. *Res Q Exerc Sport* 77: 326-339.

9. Tilden, T. 1981. The spin of the ball. In *The tennis book*, ed. M. Bartlett and B. Gillen, 281-283. New York: Arbor House.

10. Tu, J., Y. Lin, and S. Chin. 2010. The influence of ball velocity and court illumination on reaction time for tennis volley. *J Sports Sci Med* 9: 56-61.

Chapter 7

1. Bollettieri, N. 2001. *Bollettieri's tennis handbook*. Champaign, IL: Human Kinetics.

2. Bower, R., and R. Cross. 2003. Player sensitivity to changes in string tension in a tennis racket. *J Sci Med Sport* 6:120-131.

3. Brody, H., R. Cross, and C. Lindsey. 2002. *The physics and technology of tennis*. Vista, CA: Racquet Tech.

4. Collins, H., and R. Evans. 2008. You cannot be serious! Public understanding of the technology with special reference to "Hawk Eye." *Public Understand Sci* 17: 283-308.

5. Fabre, J.-B., V. Martin, J. Gondin, F. Cottin, and L. Grelot. 2012. Effect of playing surface properties on neuromuscular fatigue in tennis. *Med Sci Sports Exerc* 44: 2182-2189.

6. Groppel, J.L. 1992. *High tech tennis*. Champaign, IL: Human Kinetics.

7. Hughes, M., and S. Clarke. 1994. Surface effect on elite tennis strategy. In *Science and racket sports*, ed. T. Reilly, M. Hughes, and A. Lees, 272-277. London: Spon.

8. Johnson, C.D., and M.P. McHugh. 2005. Performance demands of professional male tennis players. *Br J Sports Med* 40: 696-699.

9. Mather, G. 2008. Perceptual uncertainty and line-call challenges in professional tennis. *Proc R Soc B* 275:1645-1651.

10. Miller, S. 2006. Modern tennis rackets, balls, and surfaces. *Br J Sports Med* 40: 401-405.

11. Whitney, D., N. Wurnitsch, B. Hontiveros, and E. Loie. 2008. Perceptual mislocalization of bouncing balls by professional tennis referees. *Curr Biol* 18: R947-R949.

Chapter 8

1. Bergeron, M.F., M.D. Laird, E.L. Marinik, J.S. Brenner, and J.L. Waller. 2009. Repeated-bout exercise in the heat in young athletes: Physiological strain and perceptual responses. *J Appl Physiol* 106: 476-485.

2. Bollettieri, N. 2001. *Bollettieri's tennis handbook*. Champaign, IL: Human Kinetics.

3. Coyle, J. Cumulative heat stress appears to affect match outcomes in a junior tennis championship. 2006. *Med Sci Sports Exerc* 38: S110.

4. Ferrauti, A, M.B. Pluim, and K. Weber. 2001. The effect of recovery duration on running speed and stroke quality during intermittent drills in elite tennis players. *J Sport Sci* 19: 235-42.
5. Galloway, S.D.R., and R.J. Maughan. 1995. Effects of ambient temperature on the capacity to perform prolonged exercise in man. *J Appl Physiol* 489: 35-36P.
6. Girard, O., G. Lattier, J-P Micallef, and G.P. Millet. 2006. Changes in exercise characteristics, maximal voluntary contraction, and explosive strength during prolonged tennis playing. *Br J Sports Med* 40: 521-526.
7. Groppel, J.L., and E.P. Roetert. 1992. Applied physiology of tennis. *Sports Med* 14: 260-268.
8. Hornery, D.J., D. Farrow, I. Mujika, and W. Young. 2007. Fatigue in tennis: Mechanisms of fatigue and effect on performance. *Sports Med* 37: 199-212.
9. Johnson, C.D., and M.P. McHugh. 2006. Performance demands of professional tennis players. *Br J Sports Med* 40: 696-699.
10. Kovacs, M.S. 2007. Tennis physiology: Training the competitive athlete. *Sports Med* 37: 189-198.
11. Lees, A. 2003. Science and the major racket sports: A review. *J Sports Sci* 21: 707-732.
12. Magal, M., M.J. Webster, and L.E. Sistrunk. 2003. Comparison of glycerol and water hydration regimens on tennis-related performance. *Med Sci Sports Exerc* 35: 150-156.
13. Mendez-Villanueva, A., J. Fernandez-Fernandez, and D. Bishop. 2007. Exercise-induced homeostatic perturbations provoked by singles tennis match play with reference to development of fatigue. *Br J Sports Med* 41: 717-722.
14. Nummela, A., H. Rusko, and A. Mero. 1994. EMG activities and ground reaction forces during fatigued and nonfatigued sprinting. *Med Sci Sports Exerc* 26: 605-609.
15. Nybo, L., and B. Nielsen. 2001. Hyperthermia and central fatigue during prolonged exercise in humans. *J Appl Physiol* 91: 1055-1060.
16. Pluim, B., and M. Safran. 2004. *From breakpoint to advantage: A practical guide to optimal tennis health and performance.* Vista, CA: Racquet Tech.
17. Reilly, T., and J. Palmer. 1994. Investigation of exercise intensity in male singles lawn tennis. In: Reilly, T., M. Hughes, and A. Lees (eds). *Science and racket sports.* London: E&F Spon, pp. 10-13.
18. Roetert, E.P., and M.S. Kovacs. 2011. *Tennis anatomy.* Champaign, IL: Human Kinetics.
19. Smekal, G., S.P. Von Duvillard, C. Rihacek, R. Pokan, P. Hofmann, R. Baron, H. Tschan, and N. Bachl. 2001. A physiological profile of tennis match play. *Med Sci Sports Exerc* 33: 999-1005.
20. Tippet, M.L., J.R. Stofan, M. Lacambra, and C.A. Horswill. 2011. Core temperature and sweat responses in professional women's tennis players during tournament play in the heat. *J Athl Train* 46: 55-60.
21. Vergauwen, L., F. Brouns, and P. Hespel. 1998. Carbohydrate supplementation improves stroke performance in tennis. *Med Sci Sports Exerc* 30:1289-95.

Chapter 9

1. Arciero, P. 2012. Personal communication.
2. Atienza, F.L., I. Balaguer, and M.L. Garcia-Merita. 1998. Video modeling and imagining training on performance of tennis service of 9- to 12-year-old children. *Percept Mot Skills* 87: 519-529.
3. Buccino, G., S. Vogt, A. Ritzl, G.R. Fink, K. Zilles, H.J. Freund, and G. Rizzolatti. 2004. Neural circuits underlying imitation learning of hand actions: An event-related fMRI study. *Neuron* 42: 323-334.
4. Coelho, R.W., W. DeCampos, S.G. DaSilva, F.H.A. Okazaki, and B. Keller. 2007. Imagery intervention in open and closed tennis motor skill performance. *Percept Mot Skills* 105: 458-468.
5. Cumming, J., and C. Hall. 2002. Deliberate imagery practice: The development of imagery skills in competitive athletes. *J Abnorm Psych* 20: 137-145.
6. Doheny, M.O. 1993. Mental practice: An alternative approach to teaching motor skills. *J Nurs Educ* 32: 260-264.
7. Ericsson, K.A. 2012. Personal communication.
8. Ericsson, K.A., K. Nandagopal, and R.W. Roring. 2009. Toward a science of exceptional achievement. *Ann NY Acad Sci* 1172: 199-217.
9. Fabbri-Destro, M., and G. Rizzolati. 2008. Mirror neurons and mirror systems in monkey and humans. *Physiology* 23: 171-179.
10. Iacoboni, M. 2005. Neural mechanisms of imitation. *Curr Opinion Neurobiol* 15: 632-637.
11. la Fougere, C., A. Zwergal, A. Rominger, S. Förster, G. Fesl, M. Dieterich, T. Brandt, M. Strupp, P. Bartenstein, and K. Jahn. 2010. Real versus imagined locomotion: A [18F] PET-fMRI comparison. *NeuroImage* 50: 1589-1598.
12. Nedelko, V., T. Hassa, F. Hamzei, C. Weiller, F. Binkofski, M.A. Schoenfeld, O. Tüscher, and C. Dettmers. 2010. Age-independent activation of the mirror neuron system during action observation and action imagery: A fMRI study. *Restor Neurol Neurosci* 28: 737-747.
13. Rizzolatti, G., and L. Craighero. 2004. The mirror-neuron system. *Ann Rev Neurosci* 27: 169-192.
14. Rizzolatti, G., and M. Fabbri-Destro. 2010. Mirror neurons: From discovery to autism. *Exp Brain Res* 200: 223-237.
15. Robin, N., L. Dominique, L. Toussaint, Y. Blandin, A. Guillot, and M. Leher. 2007. Effects of motor imagery training on service return accuracy in tennis: the role of imaging ability. *Int J Sport Exerc Psych* 5: 175-186.
16. Schuster, C., R. Hilfiker, O. Amft, A. Scheidhauer, B. Andrews, J. Butler, U. Kischka, and T. Ettlin. 2011. Best practice for motor imaging: A systematic literature review on motor imaging training elements in five different disciplines. *BMC Med* 9: 75.
17. Turella, L., A.C. Perno, F. Tubaldi, and U. Castiello. 2009. Mirror neurons in humans: Consisting or confounding evidence? *Brain Lang* 108: 10-21.
18. Van Wieringen, P.C.W., H.H. Emmen, R.J. Bootsma, et al. 1989. The effect of video-feedback on the learning of the tennis serve by intermediate players. *J Sports Sci* 7: 153-162.

19. Vogt, S., G. Buccino, A.M. Wohlschlager, N. Canessa, N.J. Shah, K. Zilles, S.B. Eickhoff, H.J. Freund, G. Rizzolatti, and G.R. Fink. 2007. Prefrontal involvement in imitation learning of hand actions: Effects of practice and expertise. *Neuroimage* 37: 1371-1383.
20. Weinberg, R. 2008. Does imagery work? Effects on performance and mental skills. *J Imag Res Sport Phys Act* 3(1):article 1. Available: www.bepress.com/jirspa/vol3/iss1/art1.
21. Williams, A.M., and N.J. Hodges, eds. 2004. *Skill acquisition in sport: Research, theory and practice.* London: Routledge.
22. Wright, M.J., and R.C. Jackson. 2007. Brain regions concerned with perceptual skills in tennis: An fMRI study. *Int J Psychophysiol* 63: 214-220.
23. Zentgraf, K., J. Munzert, M. Bischoff, and R.D. Newman-Norlund. 2011. Simulation during observation of human actions—Theories, empirical studies, applications. *Vision Res* 51: 827-835.

Chapter 10

1. Abbott, A., and D. Collins. 2004. Eliminating the dichotomy between theory and practice in talent identification and development: Considering the role of psychology. *J Sport Sci* 22: 395-408.
2. Beilock, S. 2010. *Choke.* New York: Free Press.
3. Crespo, M., and M.M. Reid. 2007. Motivation in tennis. *Br J Sports Med* 41: 769-772.4.
4. Fox, A. 2010. *Tennis: Winning the mental match.* Kearney, NE: Morris.
5. Gallwey, W.T. 1974. *The inner game of tennis.* New York: Random House.
6. Gilbert, B., and S. Jamison. 1993. *Winning ugly.* New York: Fireside.
7. Gould, D., R. Medbery, N. Damarjian, and L. Lauer. 1999. A survey of mental skills training knowledge, opinions, and practices of junior tennis coaches. *J Appl Sports Psychol* 11: 28-50.
8. Gumbrecht, H.U. 2006. *In praise of athletic beauty.* Cambridge: Harvard University Press.
9. Moran, A. 1994. How effective are psychological techniques used to enhance performance in tennis? The views of some international tennis coaches. In *Science and racquet sports,* ed. T. Reilly, M. Hughes, and A. Lees, 221-225. London: Spon.
10. Oudejans, R.D.R., and J.R. Pijpers. 2009. Training with anxiety has a positive effect on expert perceptual-motor performance under pressure. *Q J Exper Psychol* 62: 1631-1647.
11. Seligman, M.E.P. 1991. *Learned optimism.* New York: Knopf.
12. Taylor, J., and G. Wilson, eds. 2005. *Applying sports psychology: Four perspectives.* Champaign, IL: Human Kinetics.13.
13. Unierzyski, P. 2003. Level of achievement motivation of young tennis players and their future progress. *J Sports Sci Med* 2: 184-186.
14. Wallace, D.F. 2006. *Consider the lobster.* New York: Back Bay Books, pp. 141-155.

INDEX

Note: The italicized *p*, *f*, and *t* following page numbers refer to photos, figures, and tables, respectively.

ABOUT THE AUTHOR

Thomas Rowland is a pediatric cardiologist at Baystate Medical Center in Springfield, Massachusetts. He serves as a professor of pediatrics at Tufts University School of Medicine and was an adjunct professor of exercise science at the University of Massachusetts.

Rowland is the author of two books: *Children's Exercise Physiology, Second Edition,* and *The Athlete's Clock*. He has served as editor of the journal *Pediatric Exercise Science* and president of the North American Society for Pediatric Exercise Medicine (NASPEM) and was on the board of trustees of the American College of Sports Medicine (ACSM). He is past president of the New England chapter of the ACSM and received the ACSM Honor Award in 1993.

Rowland is a competitive tennis player and distance runner. He and his wife, Margot, reside in Longmeadow, Massachusetts.